TAKE JOY

A WRITER'S GUIDE TO LOVING THE CRAFT

JANE YOLEN

WRITER'S DIGEST BOOKS
Cincinnati, Ohio
www.writersdigest.com

10 09 08 07 06   5 4 3 2 1

Distributed in Canada by Fraser Direct, 100 Armstrong Avenue, Georgetown, ON, Canada L7G 5S4, Tel: (905) 877-4411. Distributed in the U.K. and Europe by David & Charles, Brunel House, Newton Abbot, Devon, TQ12 4PU, England, Tel: (+44) 1626 323200, Fax: (+44) 1626 323319, E-mail: mail@davidandcharles.co.uk. Distributed in Australia by Capricorn Link, P.O. Box 704, Windsor, NSW 2756 Australia, Tel: (02) 4577-3555.

Library of Congress Cataloging-in-Publication Data
Yolen, Jane.
  Take joy : a writer's guide to loving the craft / by Jane Yolen.
     p. cm.
  ISBN-13: 978-1-58297-385-2 (pbk. : alk. paper)
  ISBN-10: 1-58297-385-7
  1. Authorship. I. Title.
  PN147.Y55 2006   2005024431
  808'.02--dc22

Editor: Amy Schell
Designer: Grace Ring
Production Coordinator: Robin Richie
Cover Illustration: © Linda Holt Ayriss /
    Photodisc Green / Getty Images

Several of these essays have appeared in whole or in part in *The Writer, Realms of Fantasy, Highlights Chatauquah Report, Book-Links*, and online at www.janeyolen.com. "A Wish From the Winter Queen" is adapted from "The Winter Queen Speaks," first published online in *Greenman Review*. This book was first published as *Take Joy: A Book for Writers* by Kalmbach Publishing Co.

A writer has many successes.

Each new word captured.
Each completed sentence.
Each rounded paragraph leading into the next.
Each idea that sustains and then develops.
Each character who, like a wayward
adolescent, leaves home and finds a life.
Each new metaphor that, like the exact
error it is, somehow works.
Each new book that ends—and so begins.
Selling the piece is only an exclamation point,
a spot of punctuation.

ABOUT THE AUTHOR

Jane Yolen has been called America's Hans Christian Andersen (*Newsweek*) and a modern-day Aesop (*The New York Times*). Her books and stories have won many awards, including the Caldecott Medal (for *Owl Moon*), an Honor Award (for *The Emperor and the Kite*), the Nebula Award, the Christopher Medal, the World Fantasy Award, the Mythopoeic Society's Aslan Award, the Golden Kite Award, the Jewish Book Award, and many other honors. Her books and stories have been translated into fourteen languages, including Japanese, Chinese, Afrikaans, and !Xhosa.

She has also written and edited collections of poetry, short stories, and books on folklore, storytelling, and children's literature, including *Touch Magic* and *The Guide to Writing Books for Children*.

TABLE OF CONTENTS

The gloom of the world is but a shadow, and yet
within our reach is joy. Take joy!

—FRA GIOVANNI

CHAPTER

A word is dead
When it is said,
Some say.

I say it just
Begins to live
That day.

—EMILY DICKINSON

TAKE JOY

There are writers who believe that writing is agony, and that's the best anyone can say of it. Gene Fowler's famous words are quoted all the time: "Writing is easy: All you do is sit staring at a blank sheet of paper until the drops of blood form on your forehead." Or Red Smith's infamous screed: "There's nothing to writing. All you do is sit down at a typewriter and open a vein."

But by God, that's a messy way of working. And blood is extremely hard to get off of white paper.

Now, I am one of those people who makes a distinction between being a writer and being an author. A writer puts words on a page. An author lives in the story. A writer is conversant with the keyboard, the author with character.

Roland Barthes has said: "The author performs a function; the writer an activity."

We are talking here about the difference between desire and obsession, between hobby and life. But in either case, I suggest you learn to write not with blood and fear, but with joy.

Why joy?

It's a personal choice.

First of all, I am not a masochist willing to submit myself day after day to something that brings me pain. And I do mean day after day, because I write with a regularity that an octogenarian would envy. Like an athlete or a dancer, I am uncomfortable—and even damaged—by a day away from my work.

Second, one need not have an unhappy life to write tragedy. Or conversely, one need not be deliriously happy all the time to write comedy. (In fact, many stand-up comics admit to being miserable much of the time.) Shakespeare was neither a king nor a fool, not a Moor nor a Jew. He never saw a real fairy, and he was never at sea in a tempest. His life was somewhere between happy and sad, as are most authors' lives. Yet he could write tragedy, comedy, and everything between.

Authors are like actors; we get under the skins of our characters, inhabiting their lives for a while. We just don't have to live on and on with them forever. That way lies true psychosis.

I have written about dragons, mermaids, angels, and kings. Never met any up close. I have even written a murder mystery, but I did not have to murder someone in order to write it. Still—don't mess with me. After doing my research, I do know how!

Third, writing for a living is much easier than spending time in a therapist's chair. Cheaper, too. Authors get to parade their neuroses in public disguised as story. If we are lucky, we get paid for doing it. And we get applause as well. As Kurt Vonnegut said: "Writers get to treat their mental illnesses every day."

Writing fiction—and poetry—is a bit like dreaming. You can find out what is troubling you on a deeper level. That one's writing goes out and touches someone else on that same level—though differently—is one of the pieces of magic that attends to art.

But I speak of choosing joy as if it were truly a matter of choice. For some people it is not. For some, agony oils the writing machine.

So if you find that writing with pain is part of your process, I will not try to talk you out of it. After all, who am I to argue when Susan Sontag proclaims: "You have to sink down to a level of hopelessness and desperation to find the book that you can write." Or when Fran Lebowitz complains: "I just write when fear overtakes me." Or when Georges Simenon confesses: "Writing is not a profession but a vocation of unhappiness." I may consider them whiners and whingers more than writers, but it is simply their way. Just don't ask me to stand by and give them a literary Heimlich maneuver when they get a bit of plot stuck in their throats.

I contend it is not the writing that makes writers miserable. It is the emphasis on publication.

Here's another way to think of it: The etymology of the word *publish* simply means "to make public." The old "publishers" were folks who, like the old Quaker "Publishers of Truth," stood on street corners and shouted maxims into the air. Or like folk who remark loudly in parables, as the poor deranged Scot does who stands at the Mercat Cross on Market Street in St. Andrews every Sunday (and some weekdays as well)—rain or shine—babbling about his personal experiences with John Knox's joyless God. So, in a historical sense, you could read your book aloud to an audience, whether said audience was willing or unwilling to hear your work, and consider yourself published.

Or you could put something on a Web page on the Internet and invite a flame war. Or hire a printer and self-produce one thousand copies of a piece.

To do any of these means—in the literal, if not the literate sense—that one is published, though I cannot think of a university department or a National Book Award committee that would deem it so.

Of course, over the years, the word *publish* has changed in meaning. It has come to mean (we dare to hope) a book printed on fine paper, with a beautifully designed cover, an ad budget of $200,000, an eleven-city book tour, an interview on the *Today* show, a nomination for the Pulitzer or the Hans Christian Andersen or the National Book Award, and returns of under 50 percent.

Of course, that is publishing in the best of all possible worlds. I may never get any of that. You may never get any of that. All we can count on is the joy in the process of writing.

Uncovery, discovery, recovery are all part of that process.

So take the joy behind publishing's shadow. The joy in the process.

As Aidan Chambers says in a brilliant little book of essays called *Booktalk: Occasional Writing on Literature and Children*, "[R]eading is an act of contemplation. Writing is simply a part of that ritual activity. I write that I may read, and so contemplate what I have written."

Also, be prepared as you write to be surprised by your own writing, surprised by what you find out about yourself and about your world. Be ready for the happy accident. Open yourself to the numinous, to the shapes and shades of language, to that first powerful thrust of story, to the character that develops away from you (sort of like a wayward adolescent), to the surprise of the exact and perfect ending.

You are—after all—the very first reader of what you write. Please that reader. You may not have any other.

I vividly remember staying overnight at children's book writer Bruce Coville's apartment in New York City and hearing him working in the next room. First there was the tap-tap-tap of the keyboard and then a sudden explosion of laughter. It was an utterly spontaneous, joyful sound. Bruce was reading what he was writing. And loving it.

Just as vividly I remember sitting in my own writing room, up in the attic of my house, a room I alternately call the Aerie (because it's up as high as an eagle's nest) and MacDowell (because it is as far from the buzz of the household as a true writers colony). I was working on a novel about the wolf girls of Midnapore, India—two children discovered in a wolf's den in the 1920s. The section I was working on was a description of a slow passage through the great forest:

> So thick with sal trees was this particular part of the jungle that it was shady even during the day. The sun might be overhead, but we were rarely able to see it through the green, filtered light, until a single ray of sunshine would suddenly come through a rip in the fabric of leaves, reminding us that there was another world beyond and above the jungle. Dark as it was, it was not altogether gloomy, for the air was filled with the cries of rhesus monkeys and the steady rachetaracheta of the empty kerosene can fixed under the cart, with a protruding stick hitting against the wheels. The jungle was not even particularly frightening, for the noise of the stick

did its job and scared away most of the wild beasts. And when one time we heard the cough of a big cat nearby and then, suddenly ahead of us, saw a tiger with her cubs, I reached into the cart behind Mr. Welles for the two tabor drums. Rama and I pounded on them and the other men shouted, sending wave upon wave of noise into the air. The tiger vanished back into the black door of her cave, a bright red flash of meat in her mouth, and the cubs followed.

And then the phone rang.

The phone?

As intrusive as it is to read that, it was even more intrusive when it actually happened.

It took me a long moment to regain my footing in the ordinary world, a long moment to haul myself back from the green overlaced world of the sal. If there was any unhappiness in what I was doing, it was that I had been pulled back into the mundane, to the untidy piles of research books, the note cards scribbled with data, the mass of unanswered letters, the things that needed to be filed. How beautiful the sal forest had been in comparison. How real.

How real.

Perhaps that is the key. Writing takes us into another, brighter, deeper, more engaging world than the world we actually live in.

Even mediocre writing can do this.

But good writing creates—as E.L. Doctorow has put it—"not the fact that it's raining but the feel of being rained upon."

And great writing sets the reader down in inimitable worlds that become the reader—in two senses of the word: matching or embellishing the reader's mind, and then metamorphosing the reader by the incorporation of that world into his own.

What literary worlds am I talking about?

My list will not necessarily match yours, of course, but mine certainly includes: a world in which a girl falls down a rabbit hole and has adventures with a pack of cards. A world in which a water rat and his friends mess about in boats. A world in which a wizard lives backward in time. A world in which a white boy and a black man journey perilously down a river on a raft. A world in which an inexperienced ship's captain shares his cabin with a stranger. A world in which an exiled worldly French woman finds security and peace in an odd Danish religious sect.

These literary worlds are all places that have an inherent logic to them. They are never as messy as real life, which is full of loose ends and untidy relationships and mysteries that cannot be solved. Stories are controlled by minor gods—writers—who would not dare the untidiness of the actual world.

Still, much more may actually happen in a literary world than in one's own real one. When did you last converse with a large egg sitting on a wall or pull a sword from a stone? When did you last help a slave escape on a raft or ride with a toad in a motor car? When did you sit in a boat with a hungry tiger, or ride on a broomstick in a fast-paced Quidditch game? These stories grace our actual lives with their fictional realities. Like angels, they lift us above the hurrying world; they carry us in their pockets of light. How can you not approach such other worlds with joy?

Know this about being published: It is out of your hands. Even if you do everything you can think of to effect that outcome, you cannot make an editor take your work. You can go to conferences. You can take creative writing classes (though I have always wanted to see if it were possible to teach a course in noncreative writing). You can read books about writing, such as this one. You can set a work schedule on your computer and make a special place and space for your writing like my Aerie. You can travel to Yaddo and make friends there with performance artists. You can subscribe to *Publishers Weekly* and *The Writer* and *Poets & Writers* or find them in the library. You can get a B.A. or an M.F.A. or a Ph.D. in medieval lit. You can work as a day laborer, having heard that it will ready you for writing the great American novel. Or you can work as a librarian, because someone tells you that is the way to learn to write children's books. You can walk around Lower Slobovia for a year, sail across the Atlantic in a water closet, become Arnold Schwarzenegger's personal amanuensis, have intercourse with bug-eyed aliens, manage to marry a mass murderer, or murder a mass marrier. Or get thrown off the jury at the next Michael Jackson retrial. You can even—God help us—sleep with an editor. It does not—alas—guarantee a thing, though all of those are probably more effective than merely having talent or writing well.

Julian Gloag has written rather sarcastically "If I were to shoot my publisher in some nice public place with plenty of blood, I guarantee my novels would be back in print in plenty of time for the trial ... and the world would be a lot better off." It is not clear whether he means the world would be better off without his publisher or with his books. Or both.

All this may be true but rather beside the point. We are authors, not cannibals or movie stars or a member of (or sleeping with) Britain's royals. We are trying to write books, not produce products.

A couple of years ago I sat next to the finance officer of a major publishing company at an awards dinner, explaining the difference between selling books and selling toilet bowls. The bottom line on commodes, we both knew, is much better than on literature. (Pun intended.)

"Trust me," I said to him, "that if I hear anyone in publishing refer to their 'products,' it makes me want to reach for a gun." He was extremely careful with his wording after that! But—alas—if you read the latest Publishers Weekly, you will know that I am fighting a re-arguard action. The commodes seem to be winning.

However, once you have committed any words to the page and have sent your manuscript off to the publisher, it is mostly beyond your capacity to make anything happen in the publishing of your work.

Therefore, once the manuscript is in the mail—relax. Read a good book. Or read a bad book. Or read a bestseller, which is no guarantee of either. Just don't worry about it. Better yet—get busy writing something new.

Remember, as Emily Dickinson pointed out, "Publication is the Auction of the Mind of Man." (Are you cynical enough to remember that she wrote that after unsuccessfully trying to market her poems?)

Joy in writing can be akin to joy in life. If you are an Eeyore at heart, I suppose you might also be an Eeyore on the page. I am not, however, equating happy writers with happy books. You do not have to go far to see this isn't so. I have written books that make people laugh or groan, but I have also written two Holocaust novels. Serious writers do not have to have a gripe of the bowels in order to find the process of writing joyful.

Now, I am not a good flier. When it comes to planes, big planes are bad enough. But the first time I took a small hopper, from Seattle to Port Townsend to teach at the Centrum Writers Conference, I expected to be terrified. The plane could fit only three of us and the pilot. One extra passenger—I think it was Leslie Silko—insisted on coming and so had to crouch atop luggage in the rear.

I clutched the seat belt with both hands. I was prepared to lose my life—or my lunch.

But instead of being scared to death, I found the ride exhilarating. We skimmed the treetops, crossed the water, followed the grey ribbands of road, then swooped down at last onto the runway of the little Port Townsend airport, which was no more than a meadow with a wind sock at the far end.

At the worst of times, writing is like that for me: flying at just treetop level until the story or poem rises up to meet me. There is a joy when the air rushes past my wings; there is a sense of completeness when the journey is over.

I wish you all such joyous flights in your own writing. Save the blood and pain for real life where tourniquets and ibuprofen can have some chance of helping.

Do not be afraid to grab hold of the experience with both hands and take joy.

❝❞

INTERLUDE
Two Kinds of Writers

I think there are two kinds of writers: those who can talk about a project and by doing so begin to get a handle on it, and those who need to keep it secret to protect themselves from talking away all the good stuff.

Sometimes I am the one; sometimes I am the other.

My husband and I discuss family, money, politics, birdsong, and golf, and—of course—he always asks how a new book is coming.

"Words," I tell him. "It's just words."

Being too close to a piece is often worse than being too far away. Sometimes, it seems, I am the last person in the world to answer this question.

How is it coming?

I don't know.

The process is joyful, but that doesn't guarantee a good book.

How do I feel about the book? There are some strong sections, a touch of pathos, a couple of characters I like. The plot moves swiftly. But it is still just words.

Do I ever cut myself slack? Does any writer?

Then I remember a science fiction writer online who talked about what a good writer he was. He was fond of calling himself "One of the best writers in the field." I doubt many outside the field have ever heard of him. Few inside the field have, either. Fewer still have read his books.

Still, I envy him his sense of his own worth. Hardly any writers of my acquaintance have that. Most of us know when we write a good sentence or two, a couple of phrases, a line of poetry, a single character.

The rest—well, we wish we could rewrite it once more, and maybe this time get it right.

CHAPTER

Tell me the story
as it lies in your head.

—RUDYARD KIPLING,
"THE FINEST STORY
IN THE WORLD"

THE
BIRKENSTOCK MUSE

The writer's Muse wears sensible clothes, perfect for sitting in. She has on Birkenstock sandals because of all the nasty, muddy places she has to go to find ideas. She works hard and never complains, though she is rarely thanked for her part in the story, never acknowledged or given a book dedication. Her back aches and her fingers are arthritic, and she'd love a bit of chocolate but is loathe to ask. She remains all but invisible at the writer's side.

On the other hand, Imagination is an untamable creature. He comes and goes where he wants. He crosses boundaries when he wills, sits down on his haunches, and howls when he feels like it. He defecates on one's best Aubusson carpet and sharpens his sword on the Chippendale sideboard. He farts before the queen. Still, as feral as he is, everyone talks about him, desires his company, pays good money to stand in line to meet him, names him in speeches, and praises his magic.

And the Time Fairy? Come on. The Time Fairy does not exist. How could you believe otherwise? If there were such a creature as the Time Fairy, wouldn't we all have discrete packets of time left under our pillows? Deadlines would never faze us. Agents would have extra hours to read our manuscripts. Editors would have loads of time to return phone calls.

I am a writer, and I know these things. Would I lie?

We all want such characters to exist. They would make the writer's life easier, instead of the daily slog that it is.

However, if you want to wait around for the Time Fairy to visit you some morning, or for Imagination to lay his head with its mop of dark elflocks on your breast, or even have the Birkenstock Muse come with a cup of tea and a new story idea, set like a cold biscuit upon the accompanying saucer, please—be my guest.

I, on the other hand, being a professional writer, someone who makes a living writing, will do what professional writers always do. I will not wait around for inspiration but rush right into perspiration mode. I sit at my computer, fingers on the keyboard, and get to work.

Writers write.

It sounds too simple to be true, but there it is. Writers write.

Now some writers—like my novelist son, Adam Stemple—write a set number of words a day. He pushes out 1,000 minimum, rain or shine, on vacations or on the road with his band. Ray Bradbury claims he has written 1,000 words a day since he was a boy. A thousand words a day, and by the end of a year you have 365,000 words, or one mighty fat epic novel.

Some writers have settled on a daily page count. Or a chapter a day. Whichever comes first.

Some, like Sid Fleischman, make sure to leave themselves in midsentence so they are forced to return the next morning to finish it. Hemingway, too, worked this way, rather than having to face a blank page the next day.

Some, like Mary Whittington, phone a friend and have special hours where they challenge one another to free-writing, which is getting words onto the page quickly and with no forethought, no editing allowed.

Bruce Coville and Paula Danziger used to phone one another every day to read aloud what they had written, and if one of them had written nothing, the non-writer had to contribute money to a hated politician's war chest.

There are many ways to prime the writing pump, not all of them pretty. But most of them work.

And if you work at your writing every day, you will get better. Exercising the writing muscle is important, because flabbiness is as bad in a writer as it is in a runner.

Having a set routine—number of pages, number of words—is one way to work. Another important aspect is to have a proper place to do that writing.

Some writers (like me) love to write at home so they can be in their jammies all day long and be close to the stove and refrigerator. Some, like Zane Kotker, rent an office so they can be "at work." Some go off to writers colonies like Yaddo or Centrum, to be among like-minded folk. I simply named my writing room "The MacDowell Colony" and saved the money.

The great American poet Archibald MacLeish had a little one-room stone building about a hundred yards from his big, rambling colonial home in Western Massachusetts. And going to the stone study, rain or shine, snow or wind or hail, meant a major commitment to his work. He would leave wife, family, and visitors behind to work his allotted time every day.

And then there are writers like Madeleine Robins and J.K. Rowling, who have done their best work in cafés, surrounded by a babble of humanity.

Some writers turn the attic into their workspace. (I did, when teenagers and their noisy friends forced me upstairs!) Or an extra bedroom. Or a large closet. Or even a spot in the basement between the furnace and the washing machine. By claiming such a specific workspace, the writer signals to her intimates (spouse, partner, children, parents, landlord, etc.) that this is a place where real work gets done.

Of course I really agree with John Gardner in *On Becoming a Novelist*: "Write in any way that works for you: Write in a tuxedo or in the shower with a raincoat or in a cave deep in the woods."

Of course, the operative word in his advice is *write*. There is a big difference between the wannabes and the worker bees. The worker bees are the ones who get published. The wannabes just want to be published, they don't want to write.

And the punch line to this ramble is that once you start to work on a regular basis, who do you suppose takes up residence in your writing room? The Birkenstock Muse and that bad boy, Imagination.

The Time Fairy, too?

I told you. There is no such thing as the Time Fairy. If there were, people like me would write hundreds of books in a lifetime.

INTERLUDE
Sacred Hour

My friend Will Shetterly talks about his "sacred hour," that first hour when he is up and at his keyboard. He feels that if he is to write something true, it must happen then.

Not me. I need those first minutes after getting to my keyboard to prime the pump. I am nowhere near that sacred hour until I have some water flowing. By water I mean e-mails, snail mails, writing out checks. I need to clear these things out of my head—all the grit and grime and unresolved dreams—before I can write something worthy of my (your descriptive word here) talent.

In my husband's home county in West Virginia, they say water is pure after it has flowed over twenty-one stones. Now, that may be flawed science, but it's a great metaphor. Writing has to flow over those twenty-one stones, too.

CHAPTER

At the heart of the impulse to tell stories
is a mystery so profound.

—DENNIS COVINGTON,
SALVATION ON SAND MOUNTAIN

THE MYSTERY
THAT IS WRITING

Several years ago, when we were home in the States, there was a robbery in our Scottish house. One of the burglars was caught because he was seen carrying a very singular statue of a sphinx, which a passing jogger recognized as belonging to us. The jogger, an electrician, had just rewired our house and was quite familiar with the sphinx, which he'd found extraordinarily spooky. Two other men involved in the robbery got away.

While most of what they had taken was recovered, three things were not: a CD player, a nineteenth-century barometer, and an oil by a minor Scottish Victorian painter, William Pratt.

Several months later when we were back in Scotland, on the third day of our visit, we went into Edinburgh and stopped at the gallery where we had purchased the Pratt two years prior. We wanted to warn the owner about art thieves.

There was the William Pratt painting on the wall, in the very same place it had been two years before.

When informed, the owner immediately called the police. He had bid on the painting at an auction in Leeds and had not recognized it. But—alas—the paper trail had gone dead somewhere in Yorkshire. We did get the painting back, though the gallery owner was out a good deal of money.

A Scottish friend of mine, a novelist and poet, has leaped onto this story with the idea that the sphinx had engineered the downfall of the thieves. And it is true that while the sphinx was in police custody, one of the normally phlegmatic St. Andrews policemen, PC Davidson, told me he always felt he had to wash his hands after handling her. "She gives me the goose bumps," he said. Or the Scottish equivalent. However, all this constitutes is an anecdote, something to tell at cocktail parties and dinners. Much more needs to be explored in order to make this work as a story.

As fiction, my anecdote lacks a great many things: character, motivation, and theme, for starters. Nancy Willard, writing in *Telling Time: Angels, Ancestors, and Stories*, says, "Facts tell us everything and nothing."

Though my anecdote has a curious focus on the number three—three men in the gang, three things not recovered, the third day of our visit—the number is not otherwise integrated into the body of the telling. And with the rediscovery of the painting in the original gallery, the story has a great bloody coincidence without particular purpose stuck in the middle like a carbuncle on a tiara. No writer—or her editor—would countenance it for a minute. (Not to mention the smaller coincidence of the jogger having been our electrician.)

Interesting anecdotes are not fiction by themselves. They need the sandpaper touch of art. We do not revise reality. Or at least we do not revise it artfully enough, though my children tend to stand behind me and crook their fingers like quotation marks when I discourse about things in their childhood, citing "author embellishments."

Fiction is more than a recitation of facts or author embellishments. *It is reality surprised*. It shakes us up and makes us see familiar things in new ways. Fiction is like wrestling with angels—you do not expect to win, but you do expect to come away from the experience changed.

In the middle of his provocative and stirring book about the snake-handling churches in southern Appalachia, *Salvation on Sand Mountain*, Dennis Covington suddenly finds an equal holiness and mystery in the act of writing. He says: "The only eye worth talking about is the eye in the middle of the writer's head, the one that casts its pale, sorrowful light backward over the past and forward into the future, taking everything in at once, the whole story, from beginning to end." Though I would quibble about that adjective *sorrowful*, I would otherwise shout out "Amen!" to Brother Dennis's powerful witness to the mystery of story.

For mystery it certainly is. One moment not there— and the next moment realized.

I have been known to reply to the question "Where do you get your ideas?" by saying, "I don't know. The stories simply leak out of my fingertips." My fingertips, like Covington's eye in the middle of the writer's forehead, are part of the mystery.

Where do stories come from? It is a simple yet infinitely tricky question. How much easier it would be if there were some central warehouse where ideas were stored, waiting to be claimed. A lost-and-found of usable motifs. A clearinghouse for plot ideas. A place where writers could send away for story starters. But the truth is that even if such storage areas existed, what the ordinary visitor would find there would be only bits of rags and bone shanks and hanks of hair. As writers, we are peculiar archeologists. We gather the backward and forward remnants of our own and others' histories, mining the final part of that word: histories.

What we find there is always a surprise.

I found a novelette in my children's constant complaint of "it isn't fair," though it took me until they were grown-ups to write it.

I found a pun-filled series of easy-reading books in a newspaper article about a boy whose frog had just won a jumping contest.

I found a short story in an Emily Dickinson poem about the stars over Amherst.

I found a novel in a foggy walk in Montauk with my husband. Another on a gravestone in a Vermont country churchyard. A third in a horrifying documentary on the Holocaust. A fourth in a radio advertisement for wooden fencing.

Fiction, though, is more than just surprises. The writer in the midst of writing, like the penitent in the midst of prayer, finds the self falling away. Or getting out of the way. Only when we slip out of our writer bodies do we truly don the skin of story. We become one with the piece we are creating. In Gordon Dickson's wonderful phrase, we must "fall through the words into the story."

Sometimes it just happens, that sideslippage. More often, the writer has to work at turning sideways, becoming a mere shadow of authority, to let the story through.

As in good prayer, there is a victory in that disappearance of self. But, like prayer, it takes work at first.

There are, of course, two places where stories begin. One place is physical, touchable, knowable. The other lies deep in the hidden recesses of the heart.

Think of a map. It is a mere squiggle of lines on a page until—at one special moment—you see the very mountains, valleys, rivers, lakes that match those lines. So, too, a story takes place.

The Japanese have a word for it: *saku-taku-no-ki*.

Saku—the special sound a mother hen makes tapping on an egg with her beak.

Taku—the sound a chick makes tapping from within.

No-ki—the moment the tappings come together.

Saku-taku-no-ki—the instant a chick pecking on the inside and the mother pecking on the outside reach the same spot. The egg cracks open. New life emerges.

In just that way a story begins, with a physical tapping on the outside: a line of a song that won't leave your head, an article in the newspaper that strikes a chord, a fragment of conversation that loops endlessly, a photograph or painting that touches you deeply, a repeating dream. And then the answering emotion that taps within—sometimes days, weeks, years later.

The moment they come together, the story starts.

Turn off the phone. Forget the clock on the wall. Read the piece you have just written aloud so that the language, like drumsticks, beats out its own tune on your tympanum. Make yourself comfortable so you need not have excuses to get up from your desk.

When you look up again, swimming through the tide of story, you will find you are in a new country, one or two or six or ten hours from where you started.

How mysterious is this country? More mysterious and surprising than even we writers can imagine.

Diana Wynne Jones reports how events she creates in her stories and novels often come true after the fact of her writing them.

In my book *Briar Rose*, I invented an old Polish nobleman, Josef Potoki, who had been interred in several brutal concentration camps during the war but had managed to survive. In the novel he has made it his life's work afterward to tell visitors what had happened to the Jews of Poland, in a sense expiating the sins of his countrymen. Several years after the book was published, on a trip with my husband to Hamburg, I was taken around the city by an elderly German von, a man of noble lineage, who showed me sites in his city where Jews had been rounded up, expelled, murdered, shipped out. It was his life's holy work.

I had written of Potoki in *Briar Rose*: "A tall thin man ... [h]e had prominent high cheekbones that gave an Oriental cast to his eyes, and a perfectly straight nose. His mouth was large and mobile and firmer than his age demanded. He leaned on a silver-headed walking stick." Except for the silver head on the walking stick, that is a description of my Hamburg guide, a gentleman I had invented two years before.

A mysterious country, indeed.

The editor who taught me the most about writing novels is a wonderful woman named Linda Zuckerman. Until

I worked with Linda, I wrote my novels like a nervous tourist visiting an untidy continent, map and guidebook in hand. I was so careful to tread on the properly outlined paths, I never saw the life by the roadside. I gazed in awe at the cathedral; I never noticed the half-starved cats haunting the cathedral grounds. I researched the castle battlements but never heard the soughing of the wind through the broken portcullis or saw the gannet spiraling into the ocean below. Linda gave me permission to breathe, to take time in my books, to look about the landscape—both outer and inner—and finally to trust that the reader would follow, even at a leisurely pace, where I led.

Why was that advice so important? Because there is more to any story than a cathedral, than a concentration camp, than a stolen sphinx. Take a deep breath, and when you blow it out slowly, you will see your story take on its own life. Not the life that you impose upon it, but the life the story itself tells you it needs.

When our children were little, my husband and I used to take them on "Serendipity Trips." We would drive along the road, and if we came upon something that looked interesting, we would stop the car, tumble out, and investigate. That way we saw dinosaur footprints, an old carriage museum, covered bridges, a great crater. We spent hours investigating quarries and picnicking by lighthouses. We saw a beached shark giving birth, a fox hunting mice in a field, and thirty birders genuflecting to a great grey owl in a shattered tree. (Actually, they were just taking pictures, but we stopped because it looked so much like a religious ceremony as one after another moved forward quietly, knelt, took a few shots, and moved back in line.)

Dinosaur footprints in the shale along a local river are much more interesting than a museum filled with old bones. They are, somehow, more real. It is those footprints, slightly toed-in like a gigantic bird of prey; that shale, gray and flaky; that dark green river with its sunlit ripples meandering by the shale; the wind in your hair; the slate of sky overhead; a child's quick intake of breath as she puts her foot inside the dinosaur's print—that is what should go into your writing.

3

INTERLUDE
I Dream of an Eagle

Anthony Burgess once said that the dream seldom survives the first paragraph.

And Edith Wharton, quoting an old French proverb, wrote, "I dream of an eagle, I give birth to a hummingbird."

All writing is about that gap—no, that chasm—between expectation and final product. A veritable Grand Canyon. It is the very thing that induces writer's block.

I say that we writers should just expect that disappointment, not be surprised by it. Expect it, sidestep it, move on.

CHAPTER

You know your heart and soul are stapled
to that manuscript, but what we see are
the words on the paper.

—TERESA NIELSEN HAYDEN, EDITOR

READING THE
REJECTION LETTER

There is a big, sagging, unappetizing but in every rejection letter. Even the good ones.

Working writers become but-men and -women, connoisseurs of rejection. We learn how to mine the letter for information. With headlamps turned to the highest amps possible, we go forward into the dark.

Before the days of computer-generated rejection letters, it was possible to distinguish between a printed form letter and a hand-typed one signed by a real person. Alas, that small tidbit of hope is gone forever. Today all rejection letters look hand-typed, or rather all rejection letters have been laser printed.

So what do we have left in our mine, which has become a minefield for the novice?

We have coded messages.

Here is the secret decoder ring.

"DEAR AUTHOR..."

Enjoy this phrase while you can. It may be the only time an editor addresses you this way. On the other hand, you may have the last laugh. I was sent 113 printed rejection letters for my poetry the first year I was serious about sending out my work, and only three of those rejection letters contained scribbled words from a real editor. As I recall, those words were, "Thanks!" "Try us again!" and "Sorry!" Not much encouragement perhaps, to a non-writer. But I found them riveting, reading them over and over, taking sustenance from them, even admiring their brevity. I did not give up. I sold my 114th submission.

"WE HAVE READ YOUR MANUSCRIPT WITH INTEREST…"

That is not entirely true. But not entirely false, either. What is true is that some part of your manuscript has been read. Enough of it. By someone, though not necessarily an editor.

Think of it this way: Your manuscript goes into the editorial offices of XYZ Publishers, Inc. You are not one of XYZ's authors or an author they are trying to steal from ABC Publishers, Ltd. You do not have an agent, or at least you do not have a top agent. You are not a celebrity like Madonna, Billy Crystal, Tiger Woods, or even Lynne Cheney.

So where does your manuscript land? Onto a pile known as the slush pile. Now, slush is simply ed-speak for "unsolicited." Meaning no one in the XYZ Publishers, Inc. editorial office begged you to send it in. You are not the publisher's mother-in-law, girlfriend or boyfriend, best friend, tax accountant, or third cousin. You are not the editor's housemate, or first mate, or recent date. You are not even living with one of the mailroom guys. So your manuscript sits along with the three thousand other slush pile manuscripts that have come in this month, until a First Reader has time to look at it.

In fact, it may not even be opened until then. If you have enclosed a postcard to be returned to you so you know the manuscript has arrived, it may not be returned until a month or three later when the First Reader comes in to read. Save your money.

The First Reader may be a designated hit person, someone whose only job with the company is to come in two or three days a month—either alone or with other First Readers—and get through the pile as quickly as possible. In some houses there is an after-hours or weekend Reading Party, along with pizza and beer, and killer first lines are read out loud to the amusement of all. (First Readers have to take their amusements where they can.) Or the First Reader may be a secretary hoping to acquire editorial skills. Or a young person just out of college with a degree in English literature and a hunger for bad prose. (For more on the slush pile, see Teresa Nielsen Hayden's brilliantly funny and absolutely true account in "Slushkiller" at http://nielsenhayden. com/makinglight/archives/004641.html.) First Readers are never the top editors. The top editors simply do not have the time or the taste for *bad* anymore.

And bad most of the unsolicited manuscripts are. (To be fair, there are also a great number of bad manuscripts that come from mothers-in-law, girlfriends, boyfriends, best friends, tax accountants, and third cousins.) And bad manuscripts can sometimes come from previously published authors, even ones that XYZ is trying to steal. We published writers all have what are euphemistically called "trunk novels"—manuscripts that have been put away in a trunk and should never see the light of day. But published authors have to be treated with a bit more delicacy than slush pile writers. I am sorry, but that is the truth. As Willy Loman reminds us in *Death of a Salesman*, "Attention must be paid."

Years ago as a First Reader, I discovered a thousand-page opus called *The Breeze Goes On*, which took place during the War of 1812, with a heroine named Charlotte O'Meara who was being romanced by the Tarkington twins and a rumrunner called Reed Cutler. It was a serious paragraph-for-paragraph, chapter-by-chapter paraphrase of *Gone With the Wind*. I also read an ABC book that contained no pictures and only the letters A, AB, ABC, ABCD, etc. I also read a child's picture book about Peter Penis and Vicky Vagina and their friend Sammy Sperm. And a novel about a librarian who had an affair with a dog and tried to abort their child using a hanger in the bathroom of the library. Those at least were written in passable English and not by certifiable paranoid schizophrenics. Except, perhaps, for the alphabet book.

How far does a First Reader have to read to reject a manuscript? Sometimes a chapter or two, sometimes a page or two, sometimes only the first paragraph.

There is a wonderful story told about Kate Wilhelm, who not only is a fine science fiction writer but with her husband—the late, great Damon Knight—also ran the Clarion workshop for would-be writers. They used to draw a blue pen line at the end of a paragraph on the first or second or third page in a manuscript they were individually critiquing (though some of their past students still insist it was a red line, which they called "the red line of death"). "This," Kate or Damon would explain in private, "is where an editor would have stopped reading." How cruel—and how right—they were. An editor will use any excuse to reject a manuscript. There are way too many manuscripts out there. Not being able to read further—whether out of boredom, ennui, distress, or befuddlement—is the best excuse of all. It is the author's job to keep the First Reader—indeed, to keep any reader—going all the way through to the end.

"BUT..."

Uh, oh. I have never yet read a rejection letter without a *but* in the middle. I suppose there are some of them out there. However, I never got one. Nor have my many students or writer friends.

Still, I have to admit there are different kinds of *buts*. There's "but-this-stinks-so-don't-send-us-any-thing-else-ever-in-your-life." There's "but-this-be-longs-at-another-publishing-house." And there's "but-while-this-isn't-for-us-we-like-your-writing-and-hope-you-send-us-something-else." And there is every kind of *but* in between.

You have to read beyond the *but* to find out which one is yours. It's difficult to see over that terse, ugly word. It is a stopper, like a cork in a bottle. But you must read on.

"IT IS NOT RIGHT FOR OUR LIST."

Consider this: It really may *not* be right for their list. Did you send an adult book to a house that publishes only children's books? Did you send fiction to a house that publishes only nonfiction? Did you send a book on Wicca to a Christian company, or a Christmas book to a Jewish publishing house? Did you send a book set in New York City to a regional Louisiana press? Did you send a cookbook to a company that publishes only gardening manuals?

In other words, did you do your homework?

Fifteen years ago, I edited an imprint with Harcourt Brace that published children's and young adult fantasy and science fiction novels. I received picture books, nonfiction books, historicals, mysteries, cookbooks, sex books, textbooks. Not one of those was right for my list. *Really.* The line closed over ten years ago, yet I am still getting sent manuscripts, many of them inappropriate to the list I used to publish.

Do your homework.

It is important to note that "not right for our list" has also become a useless catchphrase. It may mean that your book is so bad it's not right for anyone's list, or it may mean the publisher already has as many mysteries-from-a-cat's-point-of-view books it will ever want. Or it may mean the publisher is no longer reading unsolicited manuscripts at all.

Do your homework.

And then ... do it again.

It is possible, of course, that your manuscript was mediocre, dismal, beyond the pale. You may in fact be an insensitive and illiterate bore. It is also possible that the Reader had a fight with his wife that morning. Or gets queasy reading books about spiders. (This actually happened to me.) Or just published a picture book about iguanas dancing and so doesn't want your lizard samba book. "Not right for our list" covers these things and more.

Besides, editors die, move west, become agents, start boutiques. Publishing companies get gobbled up by larger companies. Imprints are canceled. Trends shift. Demographics change. What's hot today is not tomorrow. This information is hardly secret, but it takes sleuthing, networking, keeping up.

Read *Writer's Digest*, *Publishers Weekly*, the Internet's *Publishers Lunch*. Join a workshop group, a national writers organization, or even several.

Nobody said writing was easy.

Selling your writing is even harder.

Do your homework. Don't waste your own time.

THE REAL SECRET

All that is prelude to the real secret of reading rejection letters. You must truly, deeply, viscerally believe that the editor is rejecting the book, not rejecting you. If you cannot understand the difference, you may be too thin-skinned to be in the business.

Remember the scene in *The Godfather* when a bunch of wiseguys drive off with one of their number in a car. He knows they are going to kill him. He doesn't argue. He doesn't fight. They tell him that they really like him and that the hit is not personal, just business. He understands.

You need to understand, too. Rejection in publishing is not personal. It's just business. The editor (misguided, stupid, thick, venal, unlettered, in the throes of personal problems, a company stooge—pick your favorite paranoiac reason) has said no to the story, not to you. It's just business.

Of course, at the moment you receive a rejection letter it *feels* personal. Especially if you know the editor. Especially if you have a relationship with the publishing company. Especially if you have been revising the manuscript with the editor's help. Especially if you have put your whole heart and soul in the story.

But trust me—it is just business.

So take a hot shower. Shout at the dog. Tear the letter (as I did recently) into tiny bits at the post office. Then take a deep breath—and laugh at yourself.

After all, nobody has died. All that has happened is that a story, a poem, an essay, a book has been turned down. *By one editor.*

Remember, I had 113 rejections before my first poem was taken. Madeleine L'Engle's Newbery Medal-winning novel *A Wrinkle in Time* was turned down by the first twenty-nine publishers who read it. Dr. Seuss's *To Think That I Saw It on Mulberry Street* was rejected by even more.

Publishing is not an exact science, but it is a matter of taste, of timing, of luck. And you will forget the hurt of all those rejection letters when the first acceptance letter arrives.

In the meanwhile, learn to read the rejection letters. Even hang them up in your room as I did with one from John Ciardi, who was poetry editor at *The Saturday Review*. Thankfully, he sent it after a few of my poems had already been taken for publication elsewhere, or I might have considered taking up horse training as an occupation. Sometimes "Not right for our list" is the kindest way to put things after all.

4

Dear Miss Yolen:

I'm sorry I see no way to work these into *SR*, though what to say of them, God knows. They are very accomplished poems. Of a comparable piano performance, I'd say just that—very accomplished. But not concert rank yet. I can't feel that these poems have entirely survived "literary-isms" and thereby found their own voice.

God knows, I can be wrong. Many thanks for the look.

Sincerely,
John Ciardi

P.S. Avoid the word "beauty"—it's inert.

❧ ❦ ❧
INTERLUDE
Nothing Is Lost

For a writer, nothing is lost. Research once done can be used again and again, a kind of marvel of recycling. As writers we need to be shameless about thieving from ourselves.

For example, I did two books on the Shakers—a nonfiction book called *Simple Gifts* and a novel, *The Gift of Sarah Barker*. And it is no coincidence that the round barn I discovered in my historical research, I then used as a piece of setting in the Sarah Barker book. It later found its way into my young adult science fiction novel, *Dragon's Blood*.

Good research swims upstream where it can spawn again.

CHAPTER

5

Art derives a considerable part of its beneficial
exercise from flying in the face of presumptions.

—HENRY JAMES, *THE ART OF FICTION*

THE ALPHABETICS OF STORY

A IS FOR ARCHITECTURE

A couple of years ago my husband and I built a kitchen, and I was overwhelmed by how many decisions and how much paperwork were involved before any workman picked up a hammer and nail. We had three meetings with the designer, two meetings with the contractor. We chose appliances and door handles and light fixtures and tile. We argued over color, over materials, over flooring. Should we lower the ceiling? Should we have four burners or five? Should the dishwasher go on the left of the counter, near the refrigerator, or to the right, near the range?

Writing a story and building a kitchen have much in common. The choices before one starts are infinite. Each choice after that narrows the field.

And then one day, the kitchen—and the story—are complete.

That's when you know what really went wrong!

At least in a book you still have many chances to revise. A new kitchen is as close to forever as most of us will get.

B IS FOR BELIEF

We ask our readers that they believe in our story, that the characters become as close to them as family. A dysfunctional family most times, but family nonetheless.

But before we can demand that belief of our readers, we must demand belief of ourselves.

Ask: Can I really hear these characters walking and talking? Do they have two left feet and no point of view? Do they stride out in brogans or moccasins? Do they stutter or lisp? Can they win an argument?

Do they speak to me in dreams? Do I hold conversations with them while waiting for a light to change?

Would I visit them in the hospital? Hold their hands as they die?

Would I let them marry my son or daughter? Would I allow them to take my grandchild to the zoo?

Would I confess my worst sins to them? Trust them with a secret? Challenge them with a lie?

Would I walk down a dark lane with them hand in hand?

Belief is not just a question of detail but of heart. All four chambers and the aorta as well.

C IS FOR CLARITY

I know that in adult books, ever since James Joyce, clarity has not been prized in story. In fact, I belong to a group of writers who call ourselves the Pre-Joycean Fellowship, much the way Rossetti and Holman Hunt and John Everett Millais began the Pre-Raphaelite Brotherhood.

By clarity I mean that there is the same lovely limpid quality in a good story that you find in a well-kept fish pond. Yes, there are depths in the pond and occasionally the goldfish hide there, surfacing only for food or to flash an orange tail at that flat, light sky. But when the fish rises and swims across the pool, it is somehow illumined by the water, made bigger, clearer, sweeter, more important. Perhaps I should skip directly to M for metaphor.

D IS FOR DANGER

Good stories are dangerous. Dangerous, anarchic, seductive. They change you, often forever.

I don't necessarily mean stories should splatter you with gore. Or the aftermath of sexual desire.

A great book is, by definition, challenging. Take that, bookbanners!

Sometimes, like T.H. White's *The Sword in the Stone*, the great book challenges our vocabularies and our history. Sometimes, like Robert Cormier's *The Chocolate War* or William Golding's *Lord of the Flies*, it challenges our comfortable morality. Sometimes, like James Joyce's *Ulysses*, it challenges our idea of linearity. Sometimes, like Ursula Le Guin's *Left Hand of Darkness*, it challenges our most basic gender assumptions.

The word *challenge* has gotten bad press because of book banners. But I contend we should reclaim the word and make it our own. A book should be challenging.

E IS FOR ELEVATION

And here I have two different kinds of elevation in mind.

The first is that which lifts. A good story lifts the reader above the mundane world.

Second, a good story is something that is itself lifted above real life. Let me give you an example.

When my father went off to England in World War II, my mother, baby brother Stevie, and I moved to Virginia to stay with my mother's parents. And when two years later Daddy came home, my brother did not know him, though I did. He attacked Daddy for trying to kiss Mommy, crying, "Don't you kiss my mommy, you bad man." Daddy went out and bought a box of chocolates, and Stevie let him do all the kissing he wanted after that.

Fun family story. And despite the fact that chocolates would have been in short supply in Hampton Roads, Virginia, in 1944, it was a story I wanted to tell as a children's picture book.

For years.

But I held doggedly to the real-life story, and nothing I did with it worked, until I ditched the chocolates and made the story the little girl's tale, not the baby brother's. In other words, I had to lift the story above the real world and so lift the readers as well.

F IS FOR FURNITURE

A good story, someone once said, is furniture for the mind. Some prefer comfortable sofas, other Danish modern. Some like zebra stripes on the cushions; other like their coverings plain.

But furniture is purposeful, decorative, and enhancing. It is not just there so you can bump your shins. Still it takes some sitting on until it is really comfortable.

G IS FOR GRAB BAG

Most of us have minds that are grab bags. Or compost heaps. Or in some cases, sewer lines. But a good story focuses all that messiness into bite-sized portions.

Awful metaphor?

Yes.

But we haven't reached M yet.

Where *do* stories come from? I answered that earlier in this book, but here is another way of looking at it.

Stories are around us everywhere, like fireflies, and the writer must be ready to grab them as they fly by. Use a net with a very small weave. Ideas are small—what we *do* with ideas is the large part of the equation.

However often I capture an idea, its look, its size, its wingspread is always a surprise.

As writers we must be ready for those surprises.

The way to do that is to organize your luck. In other words: Be prepared for whatever happy accidents may occur along the route of a story. It means clipping articles that interest you, even when you have not a clue what to do with them. It means buying odd books on the off chance that you may some day have need of them. It means being open to a universe of possibilities long before a story has arrived. As Louis Pasteur noted: "Chance favors the mind that is prepared."

H IS FOR HOPE

I truly believe that a great story must leave the reader with hope. Though I have to admit, I love a good cry.

Charlotte's Web certainly doesn't end with joy. But it does end with hope.

If absolutely everybody died at the end of *Moby-Dick*, who would be around to narrate? Or care?

I IS FOR IRRITATION

By this I am not talking about those everyday irritations we all suffer. A couple of years ago my furnace died a horrible death, spewing carbon monoxide (and a whole lot of soot) into the bedrooms, the bathrooms, and my husband's workroom.

But that's an annoyance. I learned nothing from it. I gained nothing, except—perhaps—a very expensive new heating system.

By irritation, I mean the kind of sand in the oyster that produces a pearl. A good story is that kind of irritant. You read it, then you cannot stop thinking about it. Eventually, your mind and heart encyst about it, and what occurs is a pearl of the soul.

J IS FOR JUGGLER

I love to watch the Flying Karamazov Brothers, the world's funniest, zaniest jugglers who can fling an amazingly odd assortment of items into the air and keep them moving in rhythm. Once I watched in a tent at Fort Worden State Park in Washington as they juggled a wet sponge, a baseball bat, a twist of hair ribbons, an orange, and a bowl of something. (Members of the audience were invited to throw anything into the mix—and did.)

A good story should be able to do that, too. Take a grieving and lonely widower, a somewhat homely but feisty spinster, a boy who wants a mother, a girl who is afraid to want a mother, a cat, a seashell, a letter. Throw them into the air. And if you are lucky, they come down as *Sarah, Plain and Tall*.

K IS FOR KALLIOPE

Well, this is a cheat, actually. We spell calliope with a C. But the Greeks used a *K*.

And since I have already done C for clarity, I am calling an exception, because *kalliope* is too swell a word not to be used.

Kalliope.

There is no good reason why a kalliope should make music. Sound maybe. Noise definitely. But not music.

However, when you are in the right mood for it, a good kalliope can pump out a song that gets you smiling. That makes you remember summer and county fairs and cotton candy and being young.

Or it can just hurt your ears.

Some stories are like that.

You may adore *Love You Forever*, but I hear it as a story about an overbearing and smothering mother who infantilizes her son and can only tell him she loves him when he is fast asleep. I also contend that she drugs his cocoa. And that when the man's baby daughter wakes up sixteen years later and finds him fondling her in her room, she will be calling 911 and going into therapy.

You may love *The Giving Tree* and hand it out like bonbons to all your special friends, but I hear only noise. To me it's not about giving but about taking, about a boy who takes and takes and takes from the only female figure in his life but never learns the gift of returning that giving. And it is about the Old Stump, as she is known at the end, the tree as enabler.

You may like *Hannibal*, believing it to be a portrait of how evil corrupts absolutely, but I threw it across the room and made a big dent in my reading room wall, which you may come and see any time you wish, because I didn't believe the ending for a moment. (Not to mention the middle.)

You may be a reader of Ludlum thrillers, psychological self-help books, New Age (sometimes called *woo-woo* or *newage*, to rhyme with sewage) stuff, or romance novels. I cannot read any of these. Really—I have tried, and I am tone-deaf to them all.

We write stories we hope have music at the heart. Sometimes it's only noise. And sometimes it's a kalliope pumping out pain for some, pleasure for others.

L IS FOR LAP

Which is where—if you're lucky enough—you first heard good stories.

But just as laps disappear when the storyteller stands up, so too a story can disappear if it is only a function of the teller and not the tale.

A child who wants to be cuddled can listen to a spirited rendition of the Brooklyn telephone book. That doesn't make the Brooklyn telephone book a good story, though it is certainly full of strange and interesting characters.

M IS FOR METAPHOR

I am tempted to ask, "What's a meta-phor?"

The answer is another M. Misdirection: We say one thing, one important and perhaps even deep thing, in terms of something else.

That's what a metaphor is. The word actually comes from the Greek word for a moving van or cart. Go to Greece, and you will be surprised at how many trucks have the word *metafora* on the side panel.

Consider how much furniture a van can move in a day.

Don't move that much in your story, or you'll have a breakdown on the highway.

Of course, I once got a letter from a child who wrote, "I love the meddlefurs in *Owl Moon*." Another M. I think the meddler in this case was the teacher. Besides, *Owl Moon* mostly has similes, not metaphors. We must be ever pedagogically correct.

Several years ago, my husband and I lived through a lifetime in ten days when we found ourselves in the middle of every parent's nightmare: the possibility of a beloved child dying. To make a long and scary story short, all the tests came back negative, but we felt at the moment that a black line had been ruled through our lives, separating what we were before the possibility of illness and what we were afterward.

I found myself understanding for the first time that as humans we live our lives through metaphor. Everything I felt during those dark days, the way I approached mortality, the way I prayed, the way I had to view the world, was in terms of metaphor. From the black line—which of course is not literal—to the dark days (we were actually in the middle of a light blush of Indian summer), to my ideas about death, to my instant-replay memories of the child who had twenty-six years earlier been in my womb, to my conversations and prayers and meditations and bargains with God. All were made up of metaphor, which John Ciardi has so wisely called "an exactly felt error."

So slowly, agonizingly, I came to understand that metaphor and its sisters—poetry and story—are as natural to humans as breathing.

The idea that metaphor is important to human thinking is not new. It was old when Aristotle said, "To make metaphors implies an eye for resemblances." And, I suppose, one might add it implies an eye for differences as well.

To make a good metaphor a writer has to be a good observer first, which, in some senses, is the measure of an educated person, whether that education took place in a schoolroom, the workroom, the trenches, or the great outdoors. In Philip Wheelwright's telling phrase: "Metaphor is a medium of fuller, riper knowing."

N IS FOR NEVERLAND

That's the place where Peter Pan and the Lost Boys live. And one lost girl who gets to do all the washing up.

You are constructing the Neverland of your choice, whether your setting looks like Hogwarts School of Witchcraft and Wizardry or New York City, whether it is a riverbank where animals picnic or the riverbank where a runaway slave climbs onto a raft. Set the parameters to match the boundaries of your heart, the real or mundane world be hanged.

O IS FOR OPINION

Keep it to yourself.

Stories—unlike politics—do not thrive on opinions. Remember Sam Goldwyn's words: "If you want to send a message, use Western Union."

Whether we like it or not, literature always carries in it the seeds of didacticism. While it entertains, it also teaches, it preaches, it contains the moral precepts (or works hard at violating the moral precepts) of the generation in which it is written.

To put it bluntly: Authors are mired in their society.

Children's literature by its nature is a didactic art form. But writers of adult books need to be aware that there is teaching going on in their books, too. We are teaching with every breath and every breath space. Some of that teaching is real stuff—gross national product and the way to make cheese out of goat milk and how many grapes to the acre for fine wine. Some of it is in relationships. Generations of young women, for example, made the choice between being Cathy of *Wuthering Heights* or Jane in *Jane Eyre* or any one of Jane Austen's marriageable maidens before they ever understood they did not have to be abused, used, or sold into marriage.

The difference is how those opinions get in the book. Make your characters speak out of their convictions, not yours.

Or write for the op-ed page.

P IS FOR PROCESS

For several years now I have had a handwritten sign over my desk that reads: "Value the process, not the product." I put it up there one New Year's to remind myself that books are not products, that what I enjoy and do in joy is the writing. If a book is a result, good for me.

I offer that sign to anyone who needs it.

Write out your own.

Pin it where you can see it when you lift your eyes from the keyboard.

Read it once a week. More often if the week is a bad one.

Q IS FOR QUESTION

There are closed-question stories and open-question stories.

Closed-question stories permit only one kind of reading. Teachers love closed-question stories. They are easy to catechize. Student responses can be graded.

Open-question stories, though, are the great ones. They are the stories that are so rich and puzzling, they leave the reader with different responses each time she goes back and rereads the tale.

R IS FOR RELIEF

Every story—whether funny or serious—needs a place where the reader can rest, take a breath, relax, sigh, put a hand to the chest, get a drink of water, use the P word.

That place may be a short stopover, an eye blink, a paragraph, or a chapter. However, don't let readers rest too long, or they'll be picking up someone else's story instead.

S IS FOR SACRED

The greatest stories touch on the sacred, that moment when head and heart and soul combine.

My "sacred" may not be yours. We may worship at different altars. My sacred story moments include Charlotte dying in *Charlotte's Web*, the cry of the wolves when Akela dies in *The Jungle Book*, the section of *Tuck Everlasting* when Winnie makes up her mind about living forever, the last sentence of *Where the Wild Things Are* because you know how much Max's mother really loves him, the place in *The Red Tent* where Dinah first meets her grandmother, Rebecca.

It is in the final speech about "A far, far better thing" in *A Tale of Two Cities*, the sight of Ahab bound eternally to his whale by the ropes of his desire in *Moby-Dick*, and in the descriptions of the water in Alice Hoffman's *The River King*. It is also—I believe—in my own book *The Devil's Arithmetic* when Rifka says to Chaya in the concentration camp, "We are all heroes here."

Sacred in story has nothing to do with organized religion or disorganized religion. I have been a member of both. It has to do with that moment you are reading and suddenly the hairs on your arms and the back of your neck rise up. The moment when you and the story ascend a level of humanity and touch the very hem of heaven.

T IS FOR TRUTH

Because telling a story truthfully is the only way to write.

Truly.

U IS FOR UNCTUOUS

Okay—a definition, unctuous means oily.

It means someone characterized by a smug, smooth pretense of spiritual feeling, especially in an attempt to influence or persuade. Think Uriah Heep, his hands wrangling together. Think of a politician at a prayer meeting. Think of Jimmy Swaggart before he was caught, or Bill Clinton after. Think of Nancy Reagan just saying no, or Linda Tripp just saying yes.

Think of authors trying to warn. Trying to convince.

Be careful.

Use good soap.

V IS FOR VELVET

A velvet voice in writing is smooth and rich in feel. It carries weight. It is luxurious, the voice of royalty, orotund, bardic, vatic. It has a fine texture. It does not cling.

It can also disguise the form below, lend regalness to poverty. One can fall into its thick nap and drown there, like a mastodon in the La Brea tar pits.

Be careful.

Sometimes good, steady flannel is better.

Or silk.

You wouldn't want to go to bed in velvet every night, would you?

W IS FOR WISDOM

I contend that good children's stories are always about the Getting of Wisdom. That's another way of saying, "Let your characters grow. Up."

And good stories for adults are about the Holding of Wisdom. Another way of saying, "Recognize you are grown up."

X IS FOR EXCITING, EXITING, EXISTENCE, EXACT

In other words, approximations of the letter X.

All stories are approximations of life. Not real, but realer.

Writing takes us into another, brighter, deeper, more engaging world than the world we actually live in. We might not want to live there, but to stay for an hour or two, a day, a week—that indeed is wonderful.

Y IS FOR YOUNG

Do you believe that writing keeps you young?

Believe it.

Z IS FOR ZERO

Have zero expectations.

Don't dream about winning a Pulitzer, making a hundred thou on your first (or thirty-first) book. Don't write any acceptance speeches for the three N's: Nebula, Newbery, and National Book Award. Don't plan your outfit for the *Oprah* show or practice crossing your legs while talking to Katie Couric. Don't expect to find

⑤ your books piled high at Borders or in the window at Barnes and Noble. Don't search amazon.com for your numbers.

Write the damn story.

Nothing else matters.

INTERLUDE
Define Writer

Define writer: someone who writes.

Define author: someone who gets published.

That works in a gross kind of way. But how about these:

A writer is someone who begins by trying to catch insights as fireflies in a jar but in the end needs to see them pinned to the page.

A writer is like a lady of the night: She does it first for love but eventually does it for money.

A writer is a mage who works his magic with images and imagination.

A writer is not a grammarian but a story-terian.

A writer is a craftsman with words, an artisan with metaphor, a plumber with characters, and a kite flier with theme.

A writer is a hollow reed through which stories are played.

A writer is the spokesman for story. A writer is the spokeswoman for story. A writer is the spokesperson for story.

Nope, the first one was best. A writer is someone who writes. All the rest defines the work.

CHAPTER

If you wish to be a writer, write.

—EPICTETUS (110 A.D.)

ADVICE

When I was growing up, I thought all adults were writers. My father was a journalist, my mother a short story writer. Their friends were all authors, and my father was president of the Overseas Press Club. More writers. We lived first in New York City, then in Westport, Connecticut. Even more writers.

If I thought about adults at all, I thought of them as writers. Of course, I knew there were teachers and doctors and librarians and butchers. (This was a long time ago!) Those were their everyday jobs. But at home, late at night, I knew all those grown-ups were scribbling away.

It came as quite a shock to me to discover, rather late in my elementary school life, that most adults were actively afraid of writing. They submitted uncomfortably to the tyranny of the white page; they were made mute by the very language that could have freed them. Many of them feared words, those slippery little things that are impossible to catch and make sense of. Many even—though this seemed unthinkable to me then, as now—hated books.

All my life I have loved stories. Relied on stories. Respected them. I love stories—not predicates. Not verbs. Not comma splices and dangling participles. Grammar teachers are wrong. Love story first, and learn the grammar of it afterward.

How long have I loved story? Since forever.

As a child I used to curl up on the window seat of our Manhattan apartment reading. Reading so absorbed me that I never even heard what went on in the street four stories below. And these stories defined me to myself. They were more than mere entertainment. They were a precursor to my adult life and concerns.

As a reader I read stories that developed me. As a writer I write to discover what I am thinking and feeling. Sometimes I write to find out how a story in my head will end. Sometimes I write because an achingly beautiful sentence has somehow found its way into my mind. And sometimes, I must admit, I write because a deadline beckons its bony finger at me.

But I write because it is a joy and a pleasure and something I must do. Not because a teacher has shown me flakes falling outside and insisted I write about it. I am my own teacher and my own window and my own falling flakes.

I write, remembering what William Faulkner once said: "I write only when I am inspired. Fortunately I am inspired at nine o'clock every morning." Smart man, Mr. Faulkner.

Many writers worry about how quickly or how slowly they write. They see this as some kind of race. Well, writers are like horsemen, really. Some climb on one horse and walk it to the finish line. Flaubert.

Some trot. Hemingway.

Some gallop. Dickens.

Some are Pony Express riders, starting on one horse, changing to a fresh one on the way. Some drive matched bays. There are even some who manage troikas—three horses, lots of reins.

Me—I am a mule train driver. I hitch twenty-four of those little suckers up to my wagon and crack the whip. If one dies along the road, I cut him out of the traces and move on.

What matters, of course, is not the pace but the finish line. No one would confuse Georges Simenon, who wrote quickly and lots, with Salinger, who did not. Yet Shakespeare was certainly fast and prolific. As was Charles Dickens, Fyodor Dostoyevsky, Isaac Asimov, Alexandre Dumas, Robert Louis Stevenson, George Sand, and Sir Walter Scott. Yet we joke all the time about prolific writers.

For example, there is the story told about Alfred Hitchcock phoning Simenon only to be told by Madame Simenon that her husband could not be disturbed as he was working on his 158th novel. "Let him finish the book," Hitchcock said. "I'll hold on."

What if George Sand—who wrote every night standing up at her desk after her lover was asleep—had had a word processor? What enormous amounts of French empurpled prose would we have had then?

What if Joyce Carol Oates wrote with a quill pen? Would she be slower? Better? Or worse?

As critics we mix up the *V* word—*versatile*—and the P word—*prolific*. We make assumptions about prolificity, liking it in nature, abhorring it in art. We confuse faculty with facility, conflate speed and speciousness, and we make assumptions that less is more in the world of letters.

But a writer should be judged by the writing produced, not by numbers. I am reminded of something F. Scott

Fitzgerald said about his novel *Tender Is the Night*: "In fact," he said, "to write it, it took three months; to conceive it—three minutes; to collect the data in it—all my life."

I often go into old bookstores or to book auctions where an illustrated volume by Randolph Caldecott or a first edition Mark Twain or anything with pictures by Kay Nielsen or Kate Greenaway or Walter Crane is sold for exorbitant prices to collectors who will encase them in plastic but never read them. And on the tables—for twenty-five cents and fifty cents—unknown, forgotten, unwanted piles and piles of old books, equally unread.

Fifty years from now, similar tables will probably contain books by all of us writing today. Still, that cannot be a concern while we write. We must simply tell our stories now, make our poems now, without the threat of dark, unvisited shelves or old books crackling with age lying on dusty fifty-cents tables and ignored even by collectors.

As we write, each of us has to believe that our books are worth a tree. That our labor—and the labor of the unremarked editors, copyeditors, book designers, printers, binders—is also worth the tree. Or worthy of that tree.

"Writing," we must also remind ourselves in Theodore Roethke's wonderful phrase, "is an act of mischief." Be Loki. Be Coyote. Be willing to stir the world's soup pot, spit at the stars, show your backside to the council, whoop in church. Nothing and everything is sacred to the writer.

At writers conferences and in M.F.A. courses, well-meaning teachers offer rules about writing, handing them down as if these rules were written on stone tablets. Never believe such charlatans. I can only give you rules about writing that I apply to myself. However, some of these are rules you may be able to adapt or adopt for yourself, so I offer them here.

WRITE EVERY DAY

I must admit, I envy obsessive journal keepers and read published diaries with an avidity that touches on voyeurism. But I have to believe that either those folks lead much more interesting lives than I do—an Admiral Peary or a Virginia Woolf or even an everyday Victorian English lady—or they lie very convincingly.

What all superior journal writers seem to share is a marvelous relationship with their surroundings. They know the background information on tables, chairs, silverware, sled dogs, pinking shears. They know without fact-checking the heritage of different kinds of snow, the proper and improper names of flowers, the family trees of bumblebees and butterflies, the dates of English nobility. I have a blind spot for that kind of learning. For example, at our Scottish house every Thursday morning the gardener takes me around and tells me the names—Latin, English, and common Scottish—of all the flowers. And every Thursday afternoon I have forgotten them. I am no better with the flowers in my Massachusetts garden. I love how they look; we have been formally introduced, but I simply cannot remember their patronymics. It is Namesheimer disease at its worst. Or perhaps a kind of flower dyslexia.

6

Writing every day does not mean one has to write in a journal. It simply means the exercising of the writing muscle. Priming the writing pump.

My late father-in-law had a cabin in the West Virginia woods. There was no running water, only a pump that needed to be primed each morning with river water. We used to visit with our children. Boots on under my nightgown, I'd pick my way around the rocks first thing in the morning, always on the lookout for snakes. I'd dip the kitchen bucket into the cold rill and haul it back full to the cabin where I used it to get the pump started.

Pouring the river water into the mouth of the pump, I would then lower the handle, lift it, lower it again. The gurgle of the unseen machinery alluded to the sympathetic magic taking place: like calling to like.

The pump would wheeze, snort, pull, the handle becoming harder and harder to push. And then suddenly water—not the river water laved into the pump, but fresh, earth-chilled, underground, sweet-as-spring water would gush forth.

Everyday writing starts that way. The old river water thrown into the pump is metaphorically your letters, revisions, journal entries—if you are so minded—shopping lists, titles, single lines of poems yet to be written.

And then that sympathetic magic takes hold. As water calls water, so words call words. Up they come from the unplumbed depths, what some call inspiration and some call talent and some call soul: sweet-as-spring new ideas. Sentences. Paragraphs. Stories. Poems. Gushing, flowing, even overflowing.

The writer's day starts.

WRITE WHAT INTERESTS YOU

For me that's actually easy. Almost everything except hard science, Brussels sprouts, and hockey interests me. And I have managed to get the first two into stories and poems anyway. Hockey still eludes me.

Too many teachers, of course, beat into student heads the truism: Write what you know.

Well, I have written about Chinese emperors, selchies, mermen, dragons, pirates, trolls, Native American horses, space-going toads, the disappearing island of Surtsey, change-ringing bells, the Wright brothers, and murderers. What I know about all of those personally comes only through research. So I would rather modify that advice: *Write about what you find interesting.* Or, as Marcie Hershman said in an article in *Poets & Writers* magazine: "We write about what it is that we need to know."

Over the years—and over my almost three hundred books—I have come upon a lot of fascinating material. Sometimes I learn it while researching for a story. Sometimes I learn it first and then find a way to put it in a story. I haunt old bookstores and pick up any book that whispers my name. What have I learned? Here is a taste:

Madame Ching, who lived in the late 1800s, was the world's greatest pirate.

The Shakers sometimes smoked marijuana.

The bridge over Niagara Falls was started by a boy and a kite.

At a concentration camp called Cheimno, 320,000 people were gassed. In all only two men escaped from the camp, and only two were found alive there at the war's end.

In Devonshire, farmers used to insist on getting their hair cut only on the waning of the moon.

Sophia Smith, who founded Smith College, had little formal education herself and used to sit on the schoolhouse steps listening to the boys studying inside.

The "Darby Ram" was George Washington's favorite song.

I love this sort of thing. It is what the world is stuffed full of. I love to find it out; I love to pass it on in new and interesting ways.

WRITE FOR YOURSELF

By this I mean that you shouldn't look outside yourself for some target audience and hope to hit it. You never will because that target keeps shifting. Fads, trends, and demographics come and go while you are only on chapter four of your novel.

The only constant in your life is you. The best audience for what you write is you—the child you were, the adult you are.

I have three children, five granddaughters, and a grandson. (Pictures on request!) As much as I love them and as well as I know them, I cannot hope to please all of them with my writing and still stay honest to my own personal truths. When my children were growing up, I did not try out my ideas on them. But I did give each of them copies of my books.

They read only what they preferred.

Now they are adults, and as far as I can tell, only my daughter reads everything I write. One son reads the science fiction and fantasy. The other smiles, thanks me, and goes off fishing.

But that is as it should be. I am not writing for them. I am writing for me.

When I write children's books, I am writing for the child I was and—in some ways—still am: a child who was an omnivorous reader, a lover of words, shy unless performing, always engaged in story. A child who would read anywhere: on the window seat overlooking Central Park, on a special rock overhanging a stream in Westport, on the bus, in front of the fireplace, in a hammock, at a party, in the subway, in the family car.

And when I write an adult book, I write for the still omnivorous adult reader I am. I write the book I want to read, the one I cannot find anywhere else. I write a book to find out what happens, just as I read a book to find out what happens.

If I can interest the child and the adult who reside inside of me, I know the novel or story or poem will have a better chance to find other readers as well.

WRITE WITH HONEST EMOTION

We all have certain emotional core truths. Some of them we know, some are hidden even from ourselves. I hold the following closely: being truthful (what an odd thing for a fabulist to say), being loyal to the people I love, the efficacy of hard work, that the goodness inside each person can be reached if found early enough, and that the greatest gift is in giving.

But sometimes other truths come through in a book, even without one's willing it. And these often take an eye other than the author's to discover them.

Three months before my mother died in 1970, she had come for a visit. During her visit, she played with her grandchildren, walked in the garden, created her endless crosswords and double acrostics, and read the manuscript of my newest picture storybook, *The Bird of Time*. In that story, a miller's son, Pieter, finds a bird that can miraculously control time—speed it up, slow it down, stop time altogether. In the story Pieter uses the bird to help rescue a king's daughter caged by a wicked giant.

Now, at that time, though my entire family knew Mother was dying of cancer, my father had begged us not to tell her. So we had this polite fiction within the family that Mother had a form of non-life-threatening Hodgkin's disease. When she finished reading my manuscript, she looked up and, with that familiar wry twist of her mouth, said to me: "Intimations of mortality, eh?"

Only then did I understand what my story was really about. I had begun writing it on the very day I had been told Mother had incurable cancer. I wanted to slow down time, or stop it altogether, to keep my mother alive. And she was telling me that—reading my story—she understood I knew she was dying. She wanted to tell me she knew it, too. It was a painful, beautiful, important moment for us both.

I also remember a fifth-grade student at the Smith College Campus School asking me why I had so many walls in my picture books.

"Walls?" I was stumped. It was something I had never noticed.

And then he enumerated them: the wall in *The Girl Who Loved the Wind*, the wall in *The Seventh Mandarin*, the stone tower in *The Emperor and the Kite*, and others, which I have now forgotten. But he was absolutely right. And then he and I and the class talked about what such walls might mean, who might be hiding behind those walls, and why the author might be the last one to understand certain truths in her own stories.

My point is that one must write with as much honesty as possible. This is not necessarily an easy or even comfortable way to write. But there are also times when the writer is not aware of what a story is really saying. The honest sword has two sharp edges.

BE CAREFUL OF BEING FACILE

The best advice ever given to me by an editor came early in my career. She said, "Do not be beguiled by your own facility." So if facility in writing is your particular gift, listen well.

I have written verse with ease since a child. I even wrote my Smith College final exam in American Intellectual History in rhyme. It was far easier than actually answering the questions. The professor, stunned at this facility, gave me an A for a C's worth of knowledge, confusing a party trick with acumen or understanding.

All writers develop certain tricks: phrases that come trippingly off the tongue, characters that commute from book to book. Think of Barbara Cartland novels or the

Goosebump series by R.L. Stine. Interchangeable sets of ciphers acting out a plot-by-the-numbers. Party tricks.

The problems that come with being a well-known writer are different, of course, from the problems that come with being a beginner. A beginning writer worries about closure, about developing skills, about getting that one big chance. A well-published writer must guard against the tendency to be facile. It is incumbent upon all of us as writers to keep stretching, to keep trying new things, never to settle for the easy, for the already done, for doing what we know we can do without breaking a mental sweat.

Over the years I have tried many different genres, partially because I have many different things to say and no one genre can handle them all. But mostly because it is important not to slip into the old party tricks.

At my thirty-fifth college reunion, we were talking about passages, about approaching serenity, about looking for new challenges. I said that I was grateful to be a writer because each new book was both a challenge and a passage. Serenity in the making of literature is not life but death.

BE WARY OF PREACHING

This is a tough one because literature is a didactic art, even when it works hard not to be. An author's own biases, prejudices, desires, hatreds—as well as the society from which he springs—all can be found in his fiction. How can it be otherwise? We authors are part of our times, and our art will always reflect it.

Children's literature especially is a didactic art form. That is, children's literature is used as a teaching tool. Even when it is not being taught in the classroom, a children's book is teaching its young reader something. Ursula Nordstrom, the great editor at Harper, said something instructional to a new writer worried about writing what had already been written. "The children," she said, "are new, though we are not."

Everything in a good book (perhaps even in a bad book) is a new truth, a new revelation to a child whose experiences are, as yet, so limited. Therefore, writers for children need to be extra careful about preaching, about filling in those empty spaces for the child.

However, do not be fooled into thinking that only books for children preach. All books carry the moral messages and the civilizing authority of the writer. As writers we may believe we are ahead of our times or behind. But we have all been formed by our times. Louisa May Alcott may have been a feminist to her neighbors, but her Jo March is, at the book's close, a bit of a disappointment by today's standards in the end. Mark Twain may have been way ahead of his contemporaries on matters of race, but many an African-American critic today finds moral fault with his presumption of a certain childishness on the part of the slave, Jim.

Still, there is a big difference between the author laboring to put a moral in a book and having a moral sense emerge organically from the plot situation and characters reacting to it.

All writers have a set of morals within them. That comes from being human.

Remember this about what you write: What you preach to one believer may make another listener guffaw. Oscar Wilde once remarked about a Dickens novel: "One must have a heart of stone to read the death of Little Nell without laughing."

Preach without the P is *reach*. I would much rather reach my audience than preach to it. In the end it is better for us both.

BE READY TO GO TOPSY-TURVY

Painters know that if they turn a picture upside down, the central shapes are better exposed. No longer concerned with the drawing—is the head on straight? Are the trees consistently green?—what comes through is the composition itself.

Now, you cannot very well turn a book upside down, or read it back to front. But you can look at its composition differently.

Take a single chapter. Reread what you have written with all the modifiers blocked out. Declare war on all adverbs. Or give your main character a change in gender—male to female, or female to male. Or shift your point of view. Or number the times you have seen through a character's eyes, then heard through her ears, then how often you have used a sense of touch, taste, or smell. This will tell you where you have stumbled or played it safe or repeated yourself. It will tell you if you have gotten under the skin of your character or used caricature instead.

Turn a prose paragraph into lines of poetry (not rhymed, but single lyrical lines bound about by white space), and you will see how you have overwritten it. Or turn a poetic piece into prose, and you will suddenly find how cryptic you have been.

When we force ourselves to go topsy-turvy, we can see anew what is on the page.

BE PREPARED FOR SERENDIPITY

The word *serendipity*, which means "a happy accident," was actually coined by Horace Walpole in his tale about "The Princes of Serendip," who made more of their luck than most of us.

How does a writer organize luck? In a variety of ways. Perhaps a file of articles or quotations. Perhaps a stack of books from a secondhand shop on various fascinating subjects. I keep photos and pictures around that seem to say, "Find my story." There is one of a bear leaning wistfully on one paw and gazing out of its cage. I've never been able to write about it. Yet. One of a Malaysian merman in a glass case I have used in both a story and a poem.

When I wrote a short story called "Epitaph," about a Schliemann-like archeologist who discovers the tomb of Merlin and uses modern methods to investigate the contents, I already had the book I needed on my shelves: *Napoleon's Glands: And Other Ventures in Biohistory.*

When I was at the halfway point in a children's science fiction novel about a runaway boy, a California earthquake, and a pair of hand-signing chimpanzees, I wanted to see chimps firsthand and watch them move. But the training center for them was in Oklahoma, a long way from my home. Just as I was trying to figure out what to do, our local newspaper had an article on two scientists, a husband-and-wife team, who had trained Washoe, one of the original hand-signing chimps. They were coming to a nearby college to give a lecture. The lecture told me nothing new, but the home movies they showed of Washoe signing to her keepers were just what I needed to complete the chapters of my book.

When I worked on a novel about the Shakers, I took a trip to a Shaker museum where, because it was off-season and I qualified as a researcher, the powers-that-be let me browse in the actual diaries of the Shakers. They had some apostate journals on the shelves as well, something I had not heard of in all of my research. I found a lot of wonderful gossip there. Gossip feeds story.

Serendipity is not so simple as luck. It is the result of a conscious forging of links. The writer becomes a participant in each act of happy accident. I had the book I needed for the Merlin story, knew the names of the primate researchers so the newspaper article leaped out at me, and had done enough research to recognize the apostate gossip.

Gestalt therapists call this the *A-ha*; scientists call it the *Eureka*.

Arthur Koestler described it as "the shaking together of two previously disconnected matrices."

An author, like any fresh-faced and eager Boy Scout, must always be prepared.

Finally, this bit of advice: When writing of angels, write like an angel. When writing of devils, work like hell.

INTERLUDE
Every New Revision

Every new revision brings a writer back to square one. We are beginners in our art every time.

I see new problems each go-round.

Each time I try to see the real pattern of the book.

There are parts of soaring loveliness. And a lot of clunkers, which I hope this time I have smoothed out. But whether the words work together smoothly, I am not yet sure.

Probably I have read it too often, worked it too often, and like overworked clay, it has some serious sagging.

I remember an assistant of mine telling me about a pottery teacher she once had. She was reworking a piece on the wheel, and the teacher came along and squished the whole thing flat.

"Never overwork s**t," said the pottery teacher.

But the question is—how do you know when the piece you are working on is excrement?

When is coprolite an important fossil?

When does coal become diamond?

Even after all this time, I am constantly fooled by hope.

CHAPTER

I want to remake the world;
anything less is not worth the trouble.

—KAREN CUSHMAN

BUILDING THE HOUSE

A number of years ago, my youngest son Jason built a house in the mountains of Colorado. He was ready to start work on it in late summer, but because of the paperwork involved, as well as permission from the town's zoning committee, the building inspector, the planning board, and a dozen others, he could not begin building until November. By then the ground was frozen hard, and to dig a foundation, Jason had to rent heaters and blowers to warm it up enough so the bulldozer could do its work properly.

By then, of course, it had begun to snow.

Writing a story is a great deal like building a house. There is all that paperwork before you even begin. Notes. Research. The jotting down of ideas. But the most important beginning step is still warming things up at ground level so you can erect your story over that important foundation—the theme. For that is what theme really is—the sub-basement of whatever tale you are planning to tell.

And by the time you are ready, it is often snowing. Bills to be paid, phone calls to return, time to go to work or walk the dog or pick up the children. An avalanche of stuff.

Of course, a story does not begin with the impulse to dig a basement. But then, neither does building a house. Jason did not say, "I have a desire for a basement." First he fell in love with a part of Colorado: the way the mountains embraced the valley, the clarity of the mountain air, the spread of stars on a winter's night, the snow-capped peaks, and the ski runs down Crested

Butte. He had gone to school there, made friends there, knew his way to the high meadows where bighorn sheep grazed and elk roamed free.

He was not thinking *basement*. He was thinking *home*.

Next he found land he could afford, drew up plans, worked with a contractor, ordered materials.

It is the same with a story. Theme is not ordinarily the first thing a writer thinks of when a story starts. Sometimes a story begins with a character. Novelist John Irving begins that way. As he says, he then tries "to think up as much action for them as possible." I occasionally begin a piece that way as well. I had the idea of a red fighting dragon when I began the short story "Cock Fight," about pit dragons on the planet Austar IV.

Sometimes a story begins with a bit of research, an anecdote heard, somebody else's history recounted. My short story "Wilding" began as a reaction to a terrible news story about teens running wild in New York City's Central Park, raping and beating a young woman jogger. One newspaper dubbed it "wilding," which became a catchword for all sorts of adolescent mob behavior.

And sometimes a story begins with a piece of plot, a *what-if*. When I wrote the short story "Mama Gone," I was wondering what it would be like if your mother were a vampire and you were the only one in your country who could stop her.

However, once the story is begun, it needs that good, solid foundation: theme. And so the theme for "Cock Fight" became a boy's avoiding brutalization in a brutal world. The theme of "Wilding," unlike the news story that began it, was about a girl's coming to respect her own mental powers rather than the pure physical sensations that her teen friends are indulging in. And "Mama Gone" is not about bloodletting but about letting go.

This does not mean that a writer is necessarily conscious of the theme as the story first develops, any more than Jason thought *basement* when he was considering *home*. We writers tend to begin by concentrating on an unfolding plot, on developing full and rounded characters, on making sure everything dovetails perfectly, that no seams show. A few writers may actually know the entire arc of their story as well as its ending before they begin. I—alas—do not. I like to plunge in and see where I am going as I get there, thereby enjoying the story as its first reader, a process one writer friend of mine calls "flying into the mist."

However, somewhere around the second draft, certainly no later than the third, it is important to understand what the theme of your story is. A story, unlike reality, can be revised. Art is not life, after all. It is a lot tidier.

Now that the basics are down, the plans drawn up, real attention must be paid to that basement.

How do you find your theme? You must ask yourself what your story is about. It's as simple as that. (Though I have to admit I am often tempted, when asked what any book is about, to reply, "About three hundred pages!") A phrase is all you need, not an entire plot summary. If you think your theme sounds banal, don't worry. Themes are like old adages: *Too many cooks spoil the broth. Don't count your chickens before they hatch.* True even though trite. It is what you have done inside the story that really counts. A trick I use is to write the flap copy for the book in my head as if I were the editor. A line or two that sells the story to the reading public.

Once you have figured out the theme, go back through the story and make sure your characters are truly acting in a way that emphasizes it. But don't overdo. Being subtle about your characters' relationship to the theme is actually better than banging your reader over the head with it. Nothing is worse than a reader with a sore head. Except perhaps a character with nothing in the head at all.

Two things to remember here. First, a story may actually have several themes. "Cock Fight" is about not only the avoidance of brutality, but also a boy's maturation. And about a boy and his dog/horse/dragon. And about the price of winning.

Second: The theme that you find interesting, important, fundamental may not be what a reader thinks the story is about at all, because readers re-create any story to suit their own needs. They re-clothe the story in their own hair shirts. Put simply: Just as we write the story we need to write, they read the story they need to read. A peculiar way to communicate, but there it is.

Some people call the theme the "meaning" of the story. Some call it the "subtext." But then, some people call a basement a cellar, or a bunker, or a foundation, or just a plain hole in the ground. Whatever we call it, it still supports the house. And from the windows in Jason's Colorado home, he could see the mountains rise in majestic splendor.

INTERLUDE
A Ringing in the Head

This is how a book or story has to start. Something rings in my head, like Great Tom. A knell.

Or sounds in my brain like a horn. A call to battle.

Sometimes two characters argue in my mind.

Sometimes it is a character tapping me on the shoulder.

Sometimes it is a vision, a picture in my head.

Only when I hear that ringing, that battle horn, that clear argument, or feel that tapping, or see that vision do I know there is a story I have to tell.

Then I must invoke the magic word. Oh, yes—there is one. All truly successful writers know it.

I shall whisper it in your ear: BIC.

It stands for Butt In Chair.

Really. Hard work is the only real magic there is ... if the book in your head is to get onto the page.

CHAPTER

8

Poets are the unacknowledged
legislators of the world.

—PERCY BYSSHE SHELLEY

WHAT IS A POEM?

My friend Patricia MacLachlan, who is not a poet—or so she insists—is a dab hand at metaphor. A few years ago she spoke about a friend of hers who was "many-fauceted," and it was an image that has stuck with me.

Because poetry is just that: many-fauceted with dozens and dozens of taps just ready to dispense a full flow.

But—not to stretch this metaphor to the breaking point—we have too often dammed up the waters. First we dam it up in the classroom, feeding kids only old heavy-handed classics or winky-daisy-flower verse. Then we dam it up in elitist magazines of unreadable small print. Or spread it like graffiti over pages of art books. What we don't do a good job at is reminding folks that poetry is alive and well and that, at its best, it is accessible to anyone who wants to listen.

Or to write it.

Think about how popular Edna St. Vincent Millay was in the 1920s, 1930s, and 1940s. Folks of all educational persuasions flocked to her readings or listened to her poetry on the airwaves. Lord Byron before her had a rock star's following. e.e. cummings was tracked by paparazzi. Robert Frost read at presidential inaugurations.

Was their poetry more accessible than that of today's poets?

Were we simply listening with ears more tuned to their rhythms back then?

Or perhaps, as Daniel Mark Epstein suggests in his recent biography of Millay, the modernist critics and poets worked hard to dismantle the nineteenth-century poetry tradition that had made poets like Byron and Yeats and Millay popular figures. So, that—in his words—"All versifying that appealed to an audience as large as Millay's would be regarded, prima facie, as sentimental fodder for the dull witted and unenlightened." (Or, might I add, for the children.) And, he further states, "[B]y the last half of the twentieth century few were left to read poetry but 'professionals' and bored, reluctant students."

Yet it is important to remember that poetry, at its most basic, is a short, lyrical response to the world. It is emotion under extreme pressure or recollection in a small space. It is the coal of experience so compressed it becomes a diamond.

So why should readers not respond to poetry, whether the line reads like Emily Dickinson's "Some say a word is dead when it is said ..." or Frost's "Two roads diverged in a wood ..." or Milton's "The brute and boist'rous force of violent men" or Shelley's "Music, when soft voices die,/Vibrates in the memory—" or my "All tales are mistakes/made true by the telling"?

The answer is—if they have not early on been taught to fear or hate poetry (drip ... drip ... drip) or to think it coy or silly or unmanly or chintzy—almost everyone can love poems in the specific, if not poetry in general.

When a writer approaches the writing of a poem, though, it is not just to set down a short line and call it poetry.

One cannot simply break up a sentence and have a poem.

Think of a subject we are all familiar with—going to the grocery store. If I simply wrote "I went to the grocery store and bought grapes," that is not a poem, though a careless reading of William Carlos Williams might make one think so. "I went to the grocery store and bought grapes" is not, in fact, much more than a bald statement of fact.

But if I wrote: "I went to the store and came home loaded with grapes and grape leaves and a dream of Greece," I am getting closer. Still, even if I broke it apart into poetic lines ...

> I went to the store
> and came home loaded
> with grapes and grape leaves
> and a dream of Greece

... it would not be a poem.

Yet.

The play on the word *loaded* is fun, but where is the poem? There needs to be more, some shape to it, some shadings, as the poet Babette Deutsch warns.

> I went to the store,
> Wal-Mart, northeast
> Of King Street and the Interstate.
> Dreaming of Greece.
> I came home with grapes and grape leaves.

Now the piece certainly has a bit of shape and shading. Details help bring out its message. But it is missing the lyrical. It has not taken its next step into poetry. There is

nothing aural in it, some wordplay that makes it sparkle.
So let's try again.

> Wal-Mart is not Greece,
> Though a wine-dark puddle
> Muddles the second row.
> I go for grapes and grape leaves,
> And wonder if the next aisle
> Displays a Golden Fleece.

Now I am having some fun. There are hidden rhymes:
Greece/Fleece, puddle/muddle, row/go. Also there is
some alliteration: go/grape/grape leaves. It is not a great
poem by any means. But it has moved from prose into
poetic possibility.

What is still missing?

I think of Babette Deutsch's "Words owe their glory,
their ugly bristliness, to the fact that they inhabit more
than one world." Long ago I had that line over my desk—
though, many moves later, it has disappeared. A poem
needs to use words in a way that doubles and triples
meanings. How about this:

> I step over the wine-dark puddle,
> And pick grape leaves
> From the shelf, one jar for three dollars,
> Wondering where are the grapes,
> The hummus, the retsina,
> The Golden Fleece?

Certainly a playfulness in the first two lines helps, mis-
leading one into thinking of the outdoors. Then the next

line sets the reader straight—we are in a grocery store. All the things purchased reflect Greece without saying the name, especially the retsina, which is a wine from that region. And then the surprise of the Golden Fleece, which uncorks this particular poetic bottle.

A poem may be rhymed or in some other special form. Using particular forms can sometimes work to compress an idea into poetry. It's rather like wrapping a plain gift with wonderful paper and ribbons.

Here is a haiku, a Japanese form with a syllabic count of 5/7/5, on that grocery store:

> I long for Hellas,
> Purchasing grapes and grape leaves.
> Wal-Mart is not Greece.

This already does a lot of what my earlier attempts could not do. Can you hear a more lyrical grace in these lines? Some of that comes from the 5/7/5 structure but not all of it. Purchasing is simply a lovelier word than bought within the context of the poem. More formal and more lyrical. And then, by putting Wal-Mart at the end, I have also given the reader a surprise.

How about trying a sonnet, a fourteen-line rhymed form that contains two stanzas—one eight lines, one six. The first eight lines set the problem, the next six come to some resolution, with a final couplet summing things up. In this instance I use the rhyme scheme abab cdcd efef gg, but that is not the only way one can rhyme a sonnet.

> All the day I longed for Greece,
> Remembering the wine-dark sea;

I thought if I could buy a piece
Of grape leaf from the grocery;
Or retsina, rough and cold
Upon the tongue, then down the throat;
Or olives black and salt and bold,
With bits of Homer I could quote.
Ah then, I'd be in Hellas sure,
The azure skies, the temples white
Where hanging from the column pure
A Golden Fleece shines in the light.
But in my heart there is no peace,
For Wal-Mart sure is not a Greece.

A few years ago there was a startling article on poetry in *The Atlantic* that said that poetry was basically an art form that only other poets were interested in reading. It made its case with a poetry M.F.A. insider's sniggle and whine and along the way managed to offend just about everyone.

One of the most egregious lines in the article had to do with "the demimonde world of light verse and children's poetry" into which, according to the author—whose name thankfully escapes me—a number of previously dignified authors had fallen. Not named but certainly counted must be poets like Eve Merriam, X.J. Kennedy, Ted Hughes, Norma Farber, Maya Angelou, John Ciardi, Nancy Willard, T. S. Eliot, Lucille Clifton, Donald Hall—all poets well known in the world of adult poetry who have, somehow, fallen from grace simply by writing light verse or poems for young readers.

The *demimonde*? Can't you just see them now, standing with their backs against the street lamps: the women in low-cut revealing dresses, open-toed shoes, a smear of red lipstick across generous mouths; the men with a bit of glitter on the collar and a dark curl teasing over the forehead, tight satin pants, and moist, open lips. All calling out in husky tones, "Hi, sailor, want to hear a children's poem? Want to hear a bit of light verse?"

Let's look a bit more at the idea that no poet should sink into this indiscrete, shadowy world.

Just because a poem is in verse does not make it bad. As Emily Dickinson wrote:

> Tell all the Truth but tell it slant—
> Success in Circuit lies
> Too bright for our infirm Delight
> The Truth's superb surprise
> As Lightning to the Children eased
> With explanation kind
> The Truth must dazzle gradually
> Or every man be blind.

As an aside, I should tell you that there is an urban legend to the effect that all of Dickinson's poetry can be sung to "The Yellow Rose of Texas." This is a canard. Not all of them can be, though this one can.

Emily Dickinson always tells the truth on the slant in her poems. We come upon truth sideways and backwards and roundabout there. That does not make the truth any less true. It just makes it more palatable. She has shown us this in hundreds of poems, rhymed poems, verse—and in this poem she tells us why she has written the way she has. "Or every man be blind." Come to think of it, that is the very essence of what poetry is. *And* it rhymes.

Also, just because a poem is light does not mean it is lightweight, as N.M. Bodecker shows in this poem:

BEAUTIFICATION

Beautification
is ideal,
but uglification
is for real.

Any writer could work on an essay using that as an epigram, an essay about what has happened to the landscape of America as oil spills, paper and plastic litter, junk cars, hospital waste, etc., dim the glory of our world. It would take us long paragraphs and hard research.

Bodecker does it in eight well-chosen words. And amuses the reader at the same time.

And just because a poem is a children's poem does not mean it is meaningless. Here is a gem by David McCord:

COCOON

The little caterpillar creeps
Awhile before in silk it sleeps.
It sleeps awhile before it flies,
And flies awhile before it dies.
And that's the end of three good tries.

This profound little poem has only one polysyllabic word—*caterpillar*, and three words with two syllables:

little, awhile, before, plus the title: *cocoon.* It is extremely simple but incredibly sophisticated in its use of repetitions. It is also the shortest possible poetic route I know, too, a deep sentiment about the shortness of life and the importance of spending that life always trying. There is not a single wrong word, not a fleshy or flashy or overblown phrase. McCord has invented his own rhyme scheme: aabbb, and that final line is a wonderful surprise, both in its rhyme and in its powerful meaning.

A poem must mean something, must have a compressed power, a lyrical line, words that play against one another. A poem should enjoy its own poetry-ness, so different from straightforward one-foot-after-another prose.

But what is a poem?

Only one way to answer that really.

WHAT IS A POEM?

> What is a poem?
> Hard work.
> A single great line.
> What we see and hear the moment before sleep
>   takes us.
> The pause between heartbeats.
> The first touch of the drumstick on the tight stretch
>   of drum
> and the slight burring after.
> A word discovered after an afternoon of trying.
> An emotion caught in the hand, in the mouth.
> Two words that bump up against one another

and create something new.

Hard work.

What is a poem?

Hard work.

Literature's soul.

A touch of lemon swab on a parched mouth.

A son who smells of sweat instead of cigarettes.

A new word, like frass, which is what the caterpillar
leaves behind.

A story compressed to a paragraph,

a paragraph squeezed to a phrase,

a phrase pared to its essence.

Hard work.

What is a poem?

Hard work.

Emotion surprised.

Throwing a colored shadow.

A word that doubles back on itself, not
     once but twice.

The exact crunch of carrots.

Precise joys.

A prayer that sounds like a curse until
     it is said again.

Crows punctuating a field of snow.

Hard work.

What is a poem?

Hard work.

The space between a hummingbird's wingbeats.

A child's meddlefurs.

A whistle too high for a dog to hear.

8

One bloody word after another after another.

The graceful ellipse of memory.

The graceful collapse of memory.

The graceful lapse of memory.

The graceless lips of memory.

Hard work.

What is a poem?

Hard work.

Hard work.

Hard work.

Hard work.

INTERLUDE
The Midlist Is a Girdle

The "midlist" is like a girdle.

Does anyone remember girdles? I do. Girdles came in three sizes: Large, Medium, and Petite.

Why, you wonder, would anyone petite need a girdle?

The fact is, they didn't. Petite was simply the smallest size available, which we mediums wore with great aplomb. No one, you see, wanted to admit to wearing a girdle labeled Extra Large.

It is all a matter of marketing.

What does this have to do with the publisher's rnidlist? Well, I ask you: Is anything labeled Bottom List going to sell?

No.

Would any publisher be silly enough to send its salesmen out to say to bookstores, "This book is positively the bottom of our list, the primordial ooze out of which all other books on our list climb"?

No.

CHAPTER

Human language is a cracked kettle on which
we beat out tunes for bears to dance to when all
the while we want to move the stars to pity.

—GUSTAVE FLAUBERT

MANY VOICES

Writing teachers speak of "finding your voice" as if the damned thing is lost somewhere: behind the desk, under the computer, in back of the commode. Whenever I hear that phrase, I am reminded of the "discovery" of America. Columbus did not *discover* America—he encountered it and the native people who already lived there. They were not lost, to be found. And neither is the story's voice.

The story's voice. That is what must be uncovered, not discovered. It is not the author's voice, but the true tone of the tale.

Perhaps nowhere can differences in story voice be so readily discernible than in the literature of the fantastic. Each has its own tone and timbre, its emphatic spots, its word choices. So I have chosen to look at a kaleidoscope of fantasy voices, using as my starting place the story idea: "The Barbarian Has Tea With the Queen." At the end of this chapter I will suggest a few non-fantastic voices as well.

THE BARDIC VOICE

The Bardic voice: used in High Fantasy, where the battles of good and evil rage across the pages, where Elfland meets the Wild Hunt. The danger is that the careless writer could also do a pratfall where she meant the grand gesture.

This is also the oracular voice, the poet's vatic voice, in full metaphoric mode; the voice that came out of the hollow caves, prophesying through the swirling mists.

It often speaks in riddles, singing with the full chesty tones of the bard. Here the writer dares the pornography of innocence, using terms like Truth and Honor and Evil without gagging on them.

The actual words in the Bardic voice are sometimes archaic, Latinate, British, sonorous. The word *grey* is frequently spelled with an *e* because it sounds and looks and feels like a different color that way. One could declaim these paragraphs; in fact, you can sing much of this prose. There is frequent use of metaphor, each "exactly felt errors," as John Ciardi called them. They are "errors" only in that a metaphor—like fantasy literature itself—is not isomorphic, i.e., point-for-point perfect like a map. A metaphor makes us feel *more* than is actually said on the page. That is what makes it perfect for poetry and for fantasy, those stepsisters who share a single father but different mothers.

The Bardic voice is full of alliteration, hyperbole. There are chants, lists, spells. Sentences often end in a full stop, the strong stress syllable that reminds the reader of the tolling of a great bell. Here voices thunder, gestures are large, emotions are heightened. This voice allows us to cant to one side and call it a cakewalk. Even the most improbable things sound Biblical in import. What is written in this voice seems true if not actual, a distinction in literature if not in law.

However, the Bardic voice does not just use big words and overblown expressions. It is only generic writing that tries to get away with catchphrases and no visual details. What is needed is for the writer to have two visions: one has to do with what is beyond and above—soul, theme, heart, subtext—and one with "muffin specificity." In other words, what exactly was served for tea?

To say simply "The barbarian had tea with the queen" is reportage of the lowest kind. That will not do.

The Bardic voice would say it this way:

> He sat on the edge of his chair, that mighty-thewed barbarian, uneasy with the soft cushion at the back, for his people always said that "comfort is the enemy of the warrior." He clutched the porcelain cup with one of his death grips. It was only by chance that he did not break the cup and spill the tea, a special blend of Angoran and Baslien leaves flavored with tasmairn seeds, down the front of his leather pants. They were his best leather trews, sewn by his favorite wife. He did not want to stain them.

Tolkien wrote: "By the making of Pegasus, horses were ennobled." Well, by the creating of the heroic Bardic voice, perhaps we are all raised up as well.

Of course, there is always a downside to this kind of writing. Remember that pratfall? Well, here it is: overstatement.

How much is too much? Let me rewrite that barbarian and queen opening into *too* much, and then it will be easy to see where it drops over into self-parody.

> He sat on the edge of the rosewood and damask chair, that mightily-thewed Barbarian from the misbegotten East where night and day are but one. He sat uneasily, for unease was his mode, or dis-ease, as his mother, whom he knew only for as long as it took to be weaned, had said to him.

"Do not grow comfortable, my child," she had warned. "Comfort is the enemy of the warrior."

So he leaned forward in the chair, clutching one of the Queen's porcelain cups, painted in a wild-rose pattern by ten-year-old virgins in the eastern factories. He clutched it with the same hand that had killed Jarak, son of Jadur, and with the same grip that had throttled Malanar, priestess of the Seven Deadly Tribes. It was only by chance that he did not snap the cup in two and spill the tea—that special blend of Angoran and Baslien leaves that his ancestors had only dreamed of, flavored with tasmairn seeds gathered at night by slaves of the sultanas. He would not have been happy doing that. That particular blend of tea could stain his leather pants—made by his second wife out of the inner thigh skin of white does—and he did not want them stained.

In other words, the tendency of the Bardic voice to go over the top can lead into disastrous overwriting—or perhaps to a shot at scripting the next fantasy miniseries. A writer needs to ask herself, what do the readers need to know? What furthers the story, the characterization, the sense of place? If the first question is to ask oneself what needs to be in the story, the second is surely: What can reasonably be left out?

THE SCHOOLBOY VOICE

Let's move on to the Schoolboy voice.

Set securely in the here-and-now (or the historical here-and-now), the Schoolboy voice is a sensible, child-like—though not childish—unabashedly innocent commentary on the fantastic swirling about it. Language tends to be plainer, less Latinate, and explanations are often offered with a kind of wink to the reader. There are fewer descriptions of clothing, lots more of food. As you can guess, this voice is used mostly in children's books.

Even when the Schoolboy voice is frightened or uneasy or unclear about what is happening, there is still that tone of jollity or naive awe, a kind of Gosh-Wow!-ness. Author and hero are on a great adventure together.

In other words, this voice proclaims a sense of continuing wonder. (Try remembering Peter Pan saying that "Death is the last great adventure.") But at the same time, with this sense of enjoyment is also a sense of total acceptance of that wonder, even within the worst, most calamitous, or fearsome part of the story.

There is also a certain amount of mischievousness in the Schoolboy voice. For one thing, the reader is usually guessing the outcome of things well ahead of the characters. And the main character's necessary vulnerability affords the author a chance to really play havoc with expectations. Bruce Coville once said that the best children's books are subversive. Certainly the books written in the Schoolboy voice should be.

Interestingly, there is often an underlying tragic tone in this voice; perhaps it is the footsteps of approaching adulthood we hear.

Of course, there is a danger with this particular voice as well, the danger of sentimentality—what I call the *Velveteen Rabbit* syndrome. The line between sentiment and sentimentality in the Schoolboy voice can be crossed too easily. This voice should come with warning signs: If there are passages in the story that make you want to sigh and say "Awwwwww"—cut them out!

Let's try that barbarian with his teacup in this voice to see how different the same basic premise can sound.

> Prince Henry sat next to his mother and stared at the barbarian who teetered on the edge of his seat, one enormous hairy hand clutching a teacup.
>
> "Excuse me," Prince Henry said, "but why don't you lean back in the chair? You look terribly uncomfortable."
>
> The barbarian grunted, a sound quite like the sound Prince Henry's prize pig made in labor. "Comfortable warrior," he said in his grunt voice, "is dead warrior."
>
> "Yes, of course. But no one is actually trying to kill you here," Prince Henry said sensibly.
>
> "He means," his mother put in tactfully, "that he must at all times be on his guard so as not to get into bad habits. And Henry, you do know about bad habits, don't you?" She smiled and poured some of the tasmairn-laced tea into the cup, never showing for a moment that she feared the barbarian might crush the cup—one of an important set sent to her by her godmother, the Sultana.
>
> Prince Henry was too young to be impressed with his mother's calm. But he knew better than to say anything more. Bad habits was a subject best left unexplored.

THE JOSEPHUS VOICE

The next voice I call Josephus, after the father of historical writers, who seemed to get fact and fantasy, rumor and reality quite mixed up. Alternate history and historical fantasy require a voice that sounds reasonable yet sings, a convincing voice that never winks or hesitates when the fantastic walks onto the scene. The Josephus voice never gives away, by wink, blink, nudge, or nodding, that here is something out of the ordinary. Which means that the author has had to do all of the research of the historical novelist … and then add one thing more. But the line where fantasy crosses over—while deliberate—must seem as real as the rest.

It takes conviction, detail, and complete knowledge of the period. Be a stone in the right place. Talk like the stone. A Victorian stone will look different from a Regency stone. Be the right stone. This is serious, true business, this magic in a historical world. And though humor may occasionally be part of it, it is humor that arises from the situation; it is not imposed on it.

Get the stone facts right, and the fancies follow.

Of course, in historical fantasy, research is a good part of the job. Yet remember that Josephus added to what he knew by guesses, rumors, folklore, and religion. History is not just history; it ends with the word *story*. The dry rota of stones is not Josephus. There is that sandpaper touch of art again, blending fact and fancy.

But can truly anything happen? Said with enough assurance in the Josephus voice and set in motion properly, the answer is a resounding yes! Still, one cannot just plop a miracle into a mob and not expect mass hysteria. So the need for the assured tones, strong research as backup, and no fear or hesitations when applying the magic.

Now, how would that barbarian and his teacup fare in the Josephus voice?

Queen Victoria stared over her teacup at her new prime minister. Her nose twitched, but she did not sniff at him. It would not do. He was the barbarian, not she. All Jews were barbarians. Eastern, oily, brilliant, full of dark magic. However long they lived in England, they remained different. She did not trust him. She could not trust him. But she would never say so.

"More tea, Mr. Disraeli?"

Disraeli smiled an alarmingly brilliant smile and nodded.

His lips moved but no words—no English words—could be heard. Across the rosewood table the queen slowly melted like butter on a hot skillet. A few more cabalistic phrases and she was re-formed into a toad.

"Yes, please, ma'am," Disraeli answered.

The toad, wearing a single crown jewel on her head, poured the tea. "Ribbet," she said clearly.

"I agree, Ma'am," said Disraeli. "I entirely agree." With a single word, he turned her back. Such small distractions amused him on these state visits. He could not say as much for the queen.

THE BOOGERMAN VOICE

Now for the Boogerman voice, the voice of the kind of dark fantasy that is all about nasty, slimy, hungry things that devour everything in their paths.

Boogerman is full of feints followed by full frontal assaults. It jabs; it lulls you with details, like what you ate for dinner and how the vegetables were cooked and what wine, full-bodied and slightly amusing, you drank, and the specialty latte served to finish the meal. And then, when you are full and ripe, it ... pops you one right in the mouth, your teeth spray out, and you feel the pulsating, greasy tentacles go down your throat till the barbs catch on your heart and slowly ... slowly pull it out.

The language tends to be plain and straightforward, confidently within the setting, until the lulling begins, at which point Boogerman often waxes poetic. Then SNAP! POW! BANG! over the top into horror.

What if those dreams are nightmares? The Booger-man's vision must still be open-eyed, detailing the horrors so the reader may see them. The thing about being a writer is that you get to select the details, and it is that selection that moves the reader at the pace you want toward your inevitable but surprising slime. Art is, at its base, just a matter of selection.

And how would Boogerman write about the barbarian and his teacup date with the queen? Maybe like this:

> The Barbarian, waist a solid 44, pecs nicely sculpted by recent days at the Uptown Gym, this week's special at twenty-five dollars if you sign up the full year, wrapped his ham fist around the dimity cup of tea carefully because the cup was frigging hot. He could smell the mint leaves and something else, maybe a touch of tasmairn? As long as there was nothing else added. Nothing, you know, illegal. Like some guys always wanted you to try. They tested you these days after every match. He couldn't afford to be ruled off. Not with the house payment coming due. And wanting to buy Jolie a real ring for putting up with him so many years.

But this Queen dame, who was fronting money for his training, was—Chappy said—an angel come from nowhere, Connecticut maybe, or Maine—wanting to be part of the action, and he had to see her for tea. She said a drink, but Chappy said not during training, though he longed for a single malt, something from Scotland where his mother, God rest her, had come from and even eighty years later had a brogue could flay the skin off your cheeks.

This Queen character wanted to know what she was buying for her cash, touch the bod a bit, he guessed. The dames who came to watch him always wanted that; Jolie wouldn't mind; she was used to it, as long as it wasn't anything serious. He smiled, glad he'd put in the new bridge so the spaces between his teeth didn't show. Turned his head slightly to look at her out of the corner of his eye, Jolie liked that, said it was cute which, given he weighed in at 288, was something he supposed.

And the Queen smiled back, only her teeth were odd, pointed like, even filed if he didn't know better. And he didn't, or wouldn't know because she leaned into him, over him, those teeth, into his throat and razoring down to his belly, slitting him open, the hot intestines falling out like so many sausages, her eyes glittering, and he never laid a hand, Jolie, he swore. Or a hold. Nothing serious at all, so who was the barbarian now?

THE DARK ANGEL VOICE

The Dark Angel voice tells of another kind of terror, with a frisson instead of a flaying. Think of *The Turn of the Screw*, where misdirection and metaphor abound. Here are no frontal attacks, but rather the soft dark comes creeping up the back stairs. This is a shadowland, full of chiaroscuro and gauze, Spanish moss and the sounds of old houses creaking.

The language is soft, almost too soft, lulling, luring, whispering. If there is a noise, it patters, scatters, skitters. This is the bedtime tale that almost puts you to sleep before it strikes terror in your heart. The nightmares are almost of your own making.

The Barbarian's hand around the teacup trembled. He was afraid. And nothing—nothing!—frightened him. But it was the big house with its unmarked doors, the plush carpet that gave no warning of footsteps, the smell of cleaning powders that disguised all other scents, a falseness that unmanned him. The Prophet had given him only one warning. "Watch your manners," he had said. But what manners? His people were not ruled by women, like the soft folk of the Dales. The Daleian Queen was late, and he had to eat alone and unserved. That was unmannerly! In his yurt, she would be beaten on the palms and the soles of her feet for such a breach.

He tried to sip the weak, yellow decoction in the cup. It tasted of yak dung but without the kick. He tried to spit it out, and it drooled down his lower lip to drop soundlessly onto the lace tablecloth, pooling like a sick dog's piss. Drooling, by the gods? Like some helpless old man. He slammed his fist on the table and made the cups rattle. It masked any sound behind him where, on the wall, a dark patch grew into the shape of wings that folded around him, slowly, unremarked. The dark shape, bending over, whispered into his ear, and he heard the sibilance before the dark claimed him completely, "No-body—NOBODY—drinks before the Queen. Where are your manners, boy?"

THE MIDTOWN MAB VOICE

Then there is the voice of the magical realist, what I call London Loki or Piccadilly Puck, or perhaps, Midtown Mab, where Faerie comes to the big city.

When fairy tales were first invented, there was more mystery in the dark woods than in any village. What magical realism has done has been to move the denizens of faerie—and especially the tricksters—into the city. And you can believe the light is different there! In that harsher light, neon and flickering, we are all forced to see with altered eyes. What was once familiar—fairies and boggles and nuggles and sprites—becomes unfamiliar when dressed in modern clothes. Yet the chaotic nature of the Fey remains the same. They are adaptable to this new environment: skyscrapers for great oaks, pavement for moss underfoot.

Midtown Mab's voice, therefore, has to combine old and new. The bardic sensibilities with the modern punk/grunge vocabulary. Chants become rap. Magic in metal is different in shape but not, perhaps, different in kind. The language is at once lush and sharp, eldritch and hip. Sly references to the Eld transmute into new references to modern signifiers. The rhythms of these books are the rhythms of MTV.

When Emily Dickinson wrote "The Robin's My Criterion for Tune," she meant that what she heard in nature repeated itself in her poetry. But once a book moves out of the natural world onto the paved streets of a city, something else needs to be the criterion for the writer's tune. So the writers using the Midtown Mab voice turn to other kinds of robins to set the parameters and meters for their literary music.

But they also like to surprise, and they use language to delude and attack deliciously.

So what criterion can I choose for a Midtown Mab version of the barbarian's tea with the queen? Perhaps the peacock's raucous call. Or the cooing of rock doves or—as we called pigeons in New York City when I was growing up—flying rats.

Grax sat uneasily on the synth-hide stool waiting for the queen. He drank tea because, after a night of barhopping, from the Wet End to the White Horse, his stomach was tied up, knotted as neatly as a sailor's rope. Running his fingers over the tensed muscles, he groaned. He could hear the tea gurgling inside, complaining like the Dee in full flood.

His face had a green tinge. The queen would notice such things. Mean and green, she'd probably say, and hit him with her fan. If he was lucky she wouldn't sing.

He took another sip out of the chipped white cup. By-the-Powers-Tetley. He could have used something stronger. Blackberry maybe. He whispered to himself:

Blackberry,
Bayberry,
Thistle and thorn,

9

You'll rue the day
That you were born.

But she'd smell it on him and say something. Her word alone could make his stomachache last a full month.

When he took his third sip, she was there, sitting on a stool next to him as if it were a throne. Her hair was gold today and piled in a high crown, her lips rowan-berry red.

"New in town, sailor?" she asked lightly. "What's a nice barbarian like you doing in a place like this?" The fan waved madly. He knew she didn't expect an answer. Not from a barbarian.

"Give us a kiss."

He did what was expected, on the cheek. But her cheek was rough, the beard already beginning to show through the rouge. It surprised him. She never used to be so careless.

"By the Green, Mab!" he said, incautiously. "I thought you could do a better job than that."

She smiled sadly at him. "'The grid is going, Grax. The Magic is failing. An old queen just doesn't have the power to fool anymore."

He put down his cup and held her hands. "It doesn't matter," he said and meant it. "It doesn't matter to me."

THE DAVE BRODER VOICE

Now, voices other than fantasy voices might include the Dave Broder voice—reportage at its best. All the ordinary who-what-when-where-why of the ordinary reporter has to be there, of course. But in addition are

Broder's wonderful, sonorous cadences, his capacity for interesting divergences and clauses, a sense of the editorial without overemphasis. All these lift this above the ordinary reportage.

> Yesterday for elevenses, the British version of coffee and doughnut time, Chesiwan Khan of Mongolia came to drink tea with her royal Britannic majesty, Queen Elizabeth, at Buckingham Palace.
>
> Khan—or The Barbarian, as he is called in the British tabloids—is hardly known outside of his own country. In fact, he's hardly known in it. But he had a message for the queen, one that he felt important enough to deliver in person.
>
> And one, obviously, the queen felt important enough to hear.

THE HEMINGWAY VOICE

Then there is the Hemingway voice, prairie flat, yet full of poetry, with its short, sharp sentences, its deliberate lack of metaphor. Hemingway's emphasis on a masculine morality is tucked into the piece, too.

> The old barbarian came home. He came home to visit the queen.
>
> The queen was not amused. The queen was never amused. But she saw the barbarian because he was strong. Because he was big. And strong. And smelly. Especially because he was smelly.
>
> The queen always loved things that smelled. She considered the barbarian a thing because he was not British. Because he was not a queen.

⑨

What he smelled of was wildness. Wildness and strength. It had been a long time, the queen thought, since they had had wildness there. In the palace. She longed for that wildness, for it had been bred out of her. Bred out generations ago. Until she met the barbarian, she did not know how much she had missed it.

Whatever voice you choose to use—and these are but a few of many choices—it will never in the end be quite good enough. Not for what you want to say.

It will only be good enough up to a point; it will only approximate what you are trying to say. As humans, even the best of us stutter. We are like children just starting to speak. But writing, when it is done well, is the language of angels: lovely to listen to, long to learn. It never fully adapts to the human tongue.

Still language is all we have to work with. So grab your kettle and start to bang on it. You can play rhythm, and hope for a symphony. Sometimes we make music despite ourselves.

INTERLUDE
Nibbled by Ducks

Often I feel as if my writing time is being slowly nibbled away by ducks. I have to fight my husband, the family, the world for writing time.

Then I read a biography about Emily Dickinson, where she's shown making tea cakes and writing letters, helping in the house, playing with her nephews and her niece, etc.

I read about Edna St. Vincent Millay, who went to parties, acted in plays, had three lovers in a single day, and still wrote.

I realize we writers must live in the real world. That means cakes, letters, bills, clogged toilets. That means reading other people's books, watching TV, doing crossword puzzles, chatting on the phone. That means taking children to school, to the orthodontist, to choir practice, to basketball games. That means working till 3, till 5, till 8, till midnight. That means vacuuming the living room of cat hairs, dog hairs, husband hairs. That means running to the grocery store, the paint store, the shoe store. That means going to the doctor, the dentist, the hair salon.

That means ... life.

Besides, without life, what is there to write about?

CHAPTER

And with that sentence I am hooked.

—NANCY WILLARD,
THE WELL-TEMPERED FALSEHOOD

BEGINNINGS AND ENDINGS

Call me Ishmael.

That is considered one of the world's greatest opening lines. It starts with a mystery. Not the declarative "My name is Ishmael." Or the sidling "The fellows call me Ishmael." But a request—or perhaps it is an order—that the narrator shall be known henceforth as Ishmael. An odd name that, but for a nineteenth-century readership, a name that immediately recalls the Biblical Ishmael—the child driven into the wilderness with his slave mother. The unwanted, forgotten, once-beloved child who threatens a dynasty. The forsaken hero. The dark brother. The other side of the Semitic coin.

But what if Dorothy Parker had written that line, instead of Herman Melville? *Call me, Ishmael.* The story of a woman in love with a man who promises to phone but doesn't.

Or if Edgar Rice Burroughs had written it? *Me Ishmael, you Jane.* A story about a feral child brought up by whales.

Or if James Joyce had written it? *Ishmael. Ishmael. Yes. And Ishmael. Yes. Ishmael. Call. And yes, yes, call.*

Or Tama Janowitz? *Call me a cab, Ishy.*

Or Isaac Asimov? *Call me Ishmael-4000B.*

In other words, it is not the opening line itself, but what it portends and what it pretends to be about. Where it leads. Where it points; what it signifies; what it sets up. It is the DNA of fiction, carrying all the genetic material for the story. Or as Jay Atkinson says, "When a writer opens a story, rolls down the white space, and hits the first line, for better or worse, the narrative course has been fixed."

But the story still has to develop.

Some writers need to begin at the beginning. They simply cannot move ahead on a story until that opening is set. They write in a linear fashion, as if they were—and they are—the story's first reader. As Anthony Burgess describes it: "I start at the beginning, go on to the end, then stop." I admit I am one of these poor fools who can be made mute by the wait for inspiration. It is a terrifying thought.

Other writers, more adventurous, simply plunge into the midst of the action and come around to the opening later. "How can I know how to start it," a friend of mine once said, "until I know what the story is about?" Which makes perfect sense, except that I cannot work that way.

Still others use the same opening line for every story, a bit like priming the pump. They figure they will go back to fix it up later. Considering my husband and I entertained guests on a thirty-one-dollar table we bought at an auction for thirty-plus years, planning originally to use it only until we could afford a better one, this mode is definitely not for me. I would end up with the same opening in twenty or thirty published stories.

So it is not how you start the beginning of a story that matters. Just as it is not the opening line itself.

Because ...

... the story still has to develop.

Besides *Moby-Dick*'s opening line, here are others I love:

When Mary Lennox was sent to Misselthwaite Manor to live with her uncle everybody said she was the most disagreeable-looking child ever seen.

   —*The Secret Garden*, by Frances Hodgson Burnett

Marley was dead, to begin with.

   —*A Christmas Carol*, by Charles Dickens

Alice was beginning to get very tired of sitting by her sister on the bank, and of having nothing to do: Once or twice she had peeped into the book her sister was reading, but it had no pictures or conversations in it, "and what is the use of a book," thought Alice, "without pictures or conversations?"

   —*Alice's Adventures in Wonderland*, by Lewis Carroll

"Christmas won't be Christmas without any presents," grumbled Jo, lying on the rug.

   —*Little Women*, by Louisa May Alcott

Spells are the hardest thing in the world to get right.

   —*Magicians of Caprona*, by Diana Wynne Jones

The first week of August hangs at the very top of summer, the top of the live-long year, like the highest seat of a Ferris wheel when it pauses in its turning.

   —*Tuck Everlasting*, by Natalie Babbitt

Now, what do these have in common besides opening favorite books of mine? They are certainly not the same size or weight. One has a central metaphor; three are succinct, almost aphoristic; two have complex dialogue; one posits a mystery; three introduce important characters and the others do not. A mixed bag.

And yet.

And yet they are each a specific invitation to continue reading, setting the hook firmly in the mouth.

Why is Mary Lennox so disagreeable-looking, and why—poor child—had she been sent to live with her uncle? And will she be transformed out of her disagreeability, and if so, how? I have to know.

So, Marley was dead. Already I want to know who Marley is and how he anchors the story. Being a sucker for a mystery, I am pulled in. And even though I will be quickly disabused of that mystery, I will stay.

I recognized myself immediately in Alice the first time I read that opening sentence. I re-recognize myself every time I reread it. Not for anything in the world will I leave this story until I finish it. It is my story.

There is a sweetness touched with the tart in the opening of *Little Women* that pulls the reader right in. And even though I am Jewish and we did not celebrate Christmas, even as a girl, when I first read that line, I knew exactly what Jo meant. I had made similar complaints—not about Christmas but about everything else—lying face down on the rug in our Manhattan apartment. Jo was my kind of girl. I was Alcott's kind of reader.

And how can any fantasy reader resist Diana Wynne Jones's first line? She has spoken a truth, plainly, in a child's voice. I expect that if there really were spells, they *would* be the hardest thing in the world to get right. So I trust the author immediately. She is being totally honest with me. That bond between writer and reader has been established so simply that unless she does something I cannot forgive (like kill off the main character too soon and without reason), I will be with her until the end.

The metaphor that opens Tuck Everlasting is so perfect, I want to pin it up over my desk to remind me what to strive for as a writer. It is a gift from Natalie Babbitt to me. It also anchors the book, suspends us and our disbelief in that same top car of the Ferris wheel for the entire length of her story.

However, the opening line—indeed, the opening paragraph of a book—is more than just an invitation. It is also a promise.

As writers we must hold to that promise. Literature is a textual act between consenting individuals. We must be true to our side of the relationship. That doesn't mean that we can't say more in that first line than is first apprehended by the reader. By the end of the story, the reader should be able to go back and say, "I now understand more about this line than I did when I first read it."

Call me Ishmael. Call me Fishmeal, if you must. But don't call me late for supper.

As for middles, for some writers they just seem to serve as a bridge between a sterling beginning and a smash ending.

I say—just tell the damn story, and be done with it.

Instead, let's turn to the story's ending. It has to be both inevitable and surprising. This is not just a happy-ever-after tacked on. The ending must be about consequence, considerations paid, and *eucatastrophe.* That last is J.R.R. Tolkien's word, and it is about the price the hero is willing to pay. Even to death itself.

If the opening line is a promise, the ending is payoff to that promise. It should leave you breathless and eager to check out the opening again to see if you understand the beginning even better this time.

Some writers actually begin there. Toni Morrison says: "I always know the ending. That's where I start."

Some writers sneak up on it.

And some writers rush to an ending like a young girl to her first lover, arms wide, lips slightly parted, the heart a drum somewhere beneath the breastbone beating out its own rhythm.

However one gets to the end, know this: It is the delivery of that DNA promise made in the first sentence. Better be sure we are satisfied when we count all the fingers and toes of the child you've brought into the world.

Here are some of my favorite endings:

Twelve voices were shouting in anger, and they were all alike. No question, now, what had happened to the pigs. The creatures outside looked from pig to man, and from man to pig, and from pig to man again; but already it was impossible to say which was which.

—*Animal Farm*, by George Orwell

In another room, Emily with the other new girls was making friends with the older pupils. Looking at that gentle, happy throng of clean, innocent faces and soft graceful limbs, listening to the ceaseless, artless babble of chatter rising, perhaps God could have picked out from among them which was Emily: but I am sure that I could not.

—*A High Wind in Jamaica*, by Richard Hughes

"The stars are thin," said Grey Brother, sniffing at the new dawn wind, "Where shall we lair today? For, from now we follow new trails."

—*The Jungle Book*, by Rudyard Kipling

So they went off together. But wherever they go, and whatever happens to them on the way, in that enchanted place on the top of the Forest, a little boy and his Bear will always be playing.

—*The House at Pooh Corner*, by A.A. Milne

Wilbur never forgot Charlotte. Although he loved her children and grandchildren dearly, none of the new spiders ever quite took her place in his heart. She was in a class by herself. It is not often that someone comes along who is a true friend and a good writer. Charlotte was both.

—*Charlotte's Web*, by E.B. White

Walking to the taffrail, I was in time to make out, on the very edge of a darkness thrown by a towering black mass like the very gateway of Erebus—yes, I was in time to catch an evanescent glimpse of my white hat left behind to mark the spot where the secret sharer of my cabin and of my thoughts, as though he were my second self, had lowered himself into the water to take his punishment: a free man, a proud swimmer striking out for a new destiny.

—*The Secret Sharer*, by Joseph Conrad

Now, what do these have in common besides ending favorite books of mine? Like the openings, they are certainly not the same size or weight. Two posit a main character suddenly indistinguishable from their compatriots, one looks forward, one backward, one sits firmly a-swivel, and one compounds the entire metaphor of the tale. A mixed bag.

And yet.

And yet each resonates a loud final knell for their story. There is surprise, but not the surprise of a joke. It is the surprise of understanding, a long sigh of recognition.

Orwell's entire parable/novel leads up to the ending, where man and pig are indistinguishable in their greed. Please notice, though, that the use of the word *already* pushes the reader further to understand that this is an ongoing process that will continue long after the covers of the book have been shut. A lesser writer would have left that word out.

It is interesting to pair the ending of *High Wind* with that of *Animal Farm* because they are both about main characters suddenly blending completely into the company in which they find themselves. But what a difference. Young Emily, who has just been rescued from pirates and who—with her "innocent" child cohorts on the boat, managed to destroy the pirates without even realizing what they were doing—is put with other "innocent faces" in a girls' school. The author's ironic stance is clear to a careful reader from these last lines. However, Orwell's final lines crash about one's skull with the insistence of a hammer.

The reason? One book (*Animal Farm*) is a parable and more insistent in its message, whereas the other is a literary novel that disguises itself as a high-sea adventure but is really about the nature of true innocence.

The end of Kipling's *The Jungle Book* is a paean to the continuity of life, so apt because that is what the animals have been training young Mowgli to understand throughout his adventures.

Milne was a Victorian/Edwardian romantic and a sentimentalist. The end of the Pooh stories encapsulates the feelings about childhood that the nineteenth and early twentieth century bred in the bone. At least in the middle-class and upper-class bones. And boy, was Milne prophetic, given the Disney-trademarked Pooh universe.

Wilbur the pig says it for all writers. Everywhere.

Joseph Conrad's ending to the short novel, *The Secret Sharer*, encapsulates the entire novel's duality, its dreamlike resistance to saying whether the sharer is a real man or the young captain's unconscious. The ending, like the book, can be read and argued either way.

Beginnings and endings remain with the reader long after the story is gone. They are powerful, emotive signs cut into the storytelling trees. Pay attention to them. Work hard on them. Ignore them at your peril. Otherwise you will get lost in the woods of your writing and never find your way home.

INTERLUDE
Not Always on the Page

Writing is not always done on the page.

Often I think about a book for years, and that thinking is rarely done at my desk. I think in the shower, on an airplane, in that moment right before sleep claims me. I think rocking a grandchild to sleep, or while listening to music.

Some days, as my husband and I drive along, jazz music blaring from the radio, I go into a kind of daze, hearing the last few pages of a novel or a story as if on a radio broadcast.

I do not write those pages down.

Three reasons, really.

First, that may not be the actual ending of the book. I am someone who does not outline but lets a story grow by setting my characters loose on their own. Often the characters end up somewhere entirely different than I had planned.

Second, what sounds good during a drive—lulled by the car and the music and my sense of setting off on an adventure—usually lies flat on the page.

And third, I cannot capture what is in my head that quickly by writing the thing down pen to paper. My hand is simply not that quick. I need to be at the keyboard.

There is a fourth reason more difficult to explain. It has to do with the fleetingness of the dream state. What I concoct in such a state is a kind of open door to the subconscious. Like any dream, it is not literal, more a suggestion of what I might mean. Probably I will have half-a-dozen of these daydream scenarios before I actually set one down.

CHAPTER

Every author does not write for every reader.

—SAMUEL JOHNSON

MIND OVER MATTER

When I mentioned to a Scottish writer friend that I was going to write about point of view, he immediately quipped: "It's an interesting topic—depending upon which way you look at it!"

Which way you look at it. In fact, point of view comes down to those six words. It is the way the author looks at or relates the story, which in turn is how we readers get to see the events that are unfolding before us. Or as Percy Lubbock wrote years ago in *The Craft of Fiction*: "... the question of the relation in which the narrator stands to the story."

Which way you look at it. I take that as a working definition of point of view. Which way you look at it is another way of asking: Who is telling the story?

Thirty years ago my husband and I took a very special trip. For nine months we camped throughout Europe and the Middle East, staying anywhere our fancy led us. We saw peacocks roaming the courtyard of a French atelier, attended sheepdog trials in Cardiff, drank wine at eighteen cents a liter in Paris, took crowded buses into the center of Rome, worked in an orchard in an Israeli kibbutz, helped roast an Easter lamb over an open pit in a taverna in Greece, played bocce with old Italian men, and went snorkeling in the Red Sea.

I sent letters home every day or two as a kind of journal. My mother bound them up for us.

Years later, whenever one of us says, "Do you remember when ..." and the other challenges that memory, out comes the trip diary.

Most of the time neither one of us remembers the events correctly. That's because two people (and, in this case, a third more-reliable narrator—the letters home) to whom the same incidents happen can have entirely different experiences. Differing points of view. Each version is, in some way, the truth, only told—as Emily Dickinson wrote—*on the slant.*

A friend of mine, poet Pat Schneider, says that writing, like dreaming, "sometimes tells us what we are not ready to hear." It is up to the writer to make that truth palatable, and one of the tools by which we do that is point of view.

In the classic texts on writing—which I have to admit I studied avidly, trying to find a way into this chapter—four main points of view are discussed: Omniscient, First Person, Limited Omniscient, and Objective.

Now, it's been years since I have given any serious thought to defining point of view. So here are some ideas about these four points of view, cribbed liberally from among others—Rebecca J. Lukens's *Critical Handbook of Children's Literature*, E.M. Forster's *Aspects of the Novel*, Walter Allen's collection *Writers on Writing*, Susan Sellars's collection *Taking Reality by Surprise: Writing for Pleasure and Publication*, and Joseph Natoli's *Tracing Literary Theory*.

OMNISCIENT

The godlike narrator tells the story from above, seeing all and knowing pretty much all as well. The narrator knows not only everything the characters know but things they cannot know, too. Third-person narrative is another name for this point of view. The viewpoint is not any character's but the author's. This is a voice that Jane Austen-like says, "It is a truth universally acknowledged …"

Novelist and children's book author Corinne Demas, who also teaches at Mount Holyoke College, told me this recently: "For me (and certainly for my writing students), the most useful kind of third-person narrator is the fly on the wall (the very extreme of Omniscient)."

"Of course," she added, "there is no 'pure' Omniscient narrator simply because there isn't room (even in a Dickens novel) to put in everything."

Most of the emotional content in Omniscient narration is demonstrated through action, though occasionally the god-narrator will simply tell the audience how a character is feeling. Simply put, in the Omniscient viewpoint, the narrator's voice is stronger than that of any of the characters.

If you were to tell a familiar tale with the Omniscient viewpoint—say "The Three Bears"—it would go something like this:

> Once upon a time in the long ago when animals could talk, there lived three bears in a forest. There was Papa Bear, and he was a big bear who loved his porridge. And there was Mama Bear who was a middle-sized bear, and she loved porridge, too. And there was Baby Bear who was just a wee bear, and he loved his porridge most of all.

I would guess that the majority of narratives are told omnisciently. Certainly the old stories used this method almost exclusively.

What do you gain by an Omniscient point of view? A grand panoramic sweep of both characters and setting. Details revealed that a single character would probably never even notice and certainly would never comment on. A kind of critical judgment on all that unrolls before the reader.

Indeed, at first glance it seems that the author has complete freedom in the Omniscient mode, for anything can be related—flashbacks, flash-forwards, and flashes of insight inward as well. Why then ever use any other device?

What do you lose when you use the Omniscient viewpoint?

The Omniscient necessarily steps back from the deepest emotional levels and has to indicate them more by action/reaction than by relating them in the hushed, personal tone that a First-Person narrative can achieve. The story is therefore less immediate and, perhaps because of that, less real. And the Omniscient author must juggle an awful lot of balls in the air. As Julian Birkett points out, "Constantly having the responsibility for where you place the focus can be quite a strain."

I use Omniscient when I need a necessary distance—sometimes an ironic distance—from my story. When I want to round out the particular world, which seems more complicated than any single character can possibly know. And if that rounding-out makes a difference to the story that I want my audience to get. I then trust that the character's responses to stimuli will be sufficient to put across his emotional state to my readers. If on occasion

I give them a bit of help—telling them that Papa Bear loves his porridge, for example—that is still within the purview of my Omniscient narration.

FIRST PERSON

This is the classic "I" point of view, where an identifiable narrator tells the story. "Call me Ishmael."

But deciding which narrator should tell the story is not always as obvious as one might think. Remember—the narrator need not always be the main character. In *Moby-Dick*, for example, Ahab and the whale are really center stage. Ishmael is only an interested bystander. However, because Ishmael is also the only one left alive at the end of the story, he becomes the logical narrator. Besides, a minor character will quite often have a more interesting take on the unfolding events, be able to see what is happening from a comfortable distance.

What happens in "The Three Bears" story, if the author uses the First-Person narrative? Well, it certainly depends on which narrator the author chooses to tell the story.

If it is Papa Bear, the telling might go like this:

I've lived in this forest my whole life, in a house my own father built. He used to tell me how it took him three weeks to cut the logs and three weeks to hew them. But after he was done, it was a real family home, right and proper. When Dad died—killed by a hunter and skinned for a rug—Mom died of grief soon after. I stayed on here alone. When I married Mama Bear, I brought her to the house to live. There's nowhere we'd rather be.

But if Mama Bear tells the story, it might sound more like this:

> Porridge. Not as easy to make as you might think. Too much salt spoils it. Too much heat spoils it. Too much stirring spoils it. But as we all love porridge for breakfast, I make it every day. I can give you the recipe if you like.

And if Baby Bear were to tell the tale:

> I had no one to play with in our little house except Mama and Papa. And I thought that was enough. Until one day ...

And if Goldilocks is the narrator:

> My mother warned me and warned me about wolves. "Do not go to bed with wolves," she would say. "Remember your cousin Emma, the one who wore that silly red cloak everywhere. Remember what happened to her!" She warned me and warned me about wolves in the forest. She never warned me about the bears.

Clearly four very different takes on a very familiar story. What makes each so different is that the "I" narrator point of view molds the tale to suit the teller. The "I" narrator focuses on different details. In the openings I have related here, Papa Bear focuses on the house and its history; Mama Bear the food; Baby Bear being an only child; and Goldilocks—ever the little egotist—blames everybody for her misadventure but herself.

The story told in First Person is intimate, but do not be beguiled by this intimacy. Remember that the narrator has chosen to reveal only certain things. Art is—after all—simply a matter of selection. What the narrator leaves out may be just as revealing as what she leaves in.

The reader of a First-Person narrative becomes perforce a kind of therapist, judging both the story and the characters through a limited pair of glasses. In reflection, Papa Bear has shown himself to be house proud and caring on one level but reveals something else in what he does not say—obviously, he has never consulted with the rest of the family as to where they would prefer to live, nor does he think it necessary to do so. There is more than a hint in this opening of a self-satisfied individual, very macho and set in his ways.

> Mama Bear takes her role as cook very seriously—she is the Julia Child of bears—but feminist theory has obviously never hit her part of the forest.
>
> As for poor Baby Bear—he has no socialization skills at all. He's going to grow up to be a computer nerd and never have a date.
>
> And then there is Goldilocks, who already sounds like a teenager. I pity her mom.

But what if some other character tells the tale, a minor functionary not actually on the scene—like Goldilocks' mom? Or a character who comes on later, such as a policeman investigating the break-in at the Bears' home? Or Baby Bear's baby-sitter coping with the cub's anxieties? Or someone who lives in the same forest, just a house or two away? Or perhaps even the house itself could tell the tale. Haven't we often said "If these walls could talk ... ?" Well, they can—in a story.

What do you gain by First-Person point of view? An up-close-and-personal (and often quirkily original) take on the story. A very original voice. The "I" narration enhances reader identification with the speaker. (Young adult writers especially love to use it for this very reason.)

The First-Person point of view can carry the reader along with its sense of intense hyperreality, with its story masquerading as autobiographical truth. (My daughter was convinced that the novel *Memoirs of a Geisha* was true until I told her I had met the author who was speaking about how he did his research. She had become so totally involved in the book, she did not notice that the author was a man.) The very presence of a named narrator relating events that he claims really happened—even when these are improbable events—makes everything seem actual and immediate.

Of course, there is a literary nearsightedness that goes along with writing in First Person. In particular, there are limits to what the "I" narrator can possibly know or see or overhear behind the arras, a dangerous place as Shakespeare has warned us. This means that there are limits as well for the reader. If the viewpoint narrator is in this room eating porridge, he cannot also be out watching Goldilocks walking in the woods. Simply put: The "I" character cannot be in two places at once. (Okay—who is the wise guy who is going to point out that a novel about clones or empaths could do that very thing?)

To particularize this problem: The Bear family narrators cannot know that Goldilocks had been warned by her mother—unless Goldilocks takes time in the story to tell them. They do not know anything about her backstory, and in most basic tellings, they do not care. They can only know the results of her housebreaking—porridge eaten, chair destroyed, bed slept in. They cannot know why she has done these things; they just want her out of their home. On the other hand, if Goldilocks is the narrator, she cannot know anything about the Bears other than what she sees in their house. Not even that they like porridge and have gone for a walk. Though if she wants to, she might make some educated guesses from the up-to-date kitchen, the Stickley furniture, the handmade quilts on the beds, the photos of ursine relatives on the wall.

This particular limitation, this ego-driven narration, has led at least one critic in *School Library Journal* to characterize First-Person point of view as a "recitation of grievances, delivered by a whining narrator of limited vocabulary and experience." Obviously not what one could say about the god-like narrator of the Omniscient point of view.

The critic's complaint also points out another pitfall of the "I" narration. To be effective, the story told has to be within the knowledge boundaries and vocabulary of the narrator. Baby Bear cannot suddenly sound like a grown-up aardvark. He cannot understand philosophy, economics, the gross income of Forest Products, Inc. As long as he is Baby Bear, there are limits to what he knows. As well, Goldilocks cannot discourse on the biological imperative or the sleeping habits of bears unless she arrives at the house as an investigator or a writer for a magazine like *Nature*. What the characters say—and how they say it (the voice of the "I" narrator is particularly critical)—has to be compatible with their age, personality, and background.

Anthony Trollope also pointed out another flaw in the "I" narration. He wrote, "It is always dangerous to write from the point of 'I.' The reader is unconsciously taught to feel that the writer is glorifying himself and rebels against the self-praise. Or otherwise," Trollope adds, "the 'I' is pretentiously humble and offends from exactly the other point of view."

Clearly, then, both Omniscient and First Person have strengths and weaknesses. Personally, this author likes to use the "I" when I feel it gives my readers that wonderfully quirky and individual take on the story that I could not otherwise catch. Still, it is a more difficult voice to be successful in. Keeping the voice consistent and the character both believable and fascinating becomes a major task.

LIMITED OMNISCIENT

So let's turn then to the Limited Omniscient, which sounds—you must admit—like an oxymoron. For surely omniscience can have no limits put upon it.

Limited Omniscient combines both First Person and Omniscient by seeing things from the overview third-person narration but follows closely the thoughts, feelings, and significant backstory of one particular character. The narrator is actually the author, but he centers the story on one character. In this way the writer is both inside and alongside the character at one and the same time, a kind of literary having your cake and eating it, too.

> Once upon a time, in the long ago when animals could talk, there lived three bears in the forest. There was Papa Bear, and he was a big bear who loved his porridge. And there was Mama Bear, who was a middle-sized bear, and she loved porridge, too. And there was Baby Bear, who didn't like porridge at all. In fact, he found it incredibly gummy, and it stuck to the roof of his mouth and made it hard for him to swallow. But he never had the courage to tell the other bears so. He was, after all, only a wee bear.

OBJECTIVE

Finally, there is the Objective viewpoint: Here the writer does not enter into the minds of any of the characters at all but rather lets the action and dialogue speak for themselves. This sort of thing is usual in plays; the other term for this point of view is the "dramatic" viewpoint. It is not often used for fiction. In this approach, the reader (or playgoer) draws inferences about the emotional life of the players from what is seen or heard directly, or indirectly, in actions/reactions by the characters.

Modern art, black-on-black paintings, or repeating soup cans are the images that come to mind. The viewer has to make of them what he will, often investing more in the piece of art than the artist ever put there.

> Once in a forest lived three bears. The largest was called Papa Bear, the middle-sized one Mama Bear, and the littlest was Baby Bear.

> One day they sat down for a breakfast of porridge. Papa Bear put down his spoon. "The porridge," he said, "is much too hot."

This kind of bare-boned narration makes fairly heavy demands on the reader. Did Papa Bear set down his spoon with a bang? Or did he set it down with infinite care? Or with a sigh? Or a giggle? Or with controlled anger? Was the porridge really too hot—or was he just in a bad mood? Any action related by the author will yield a clue. And from those minimal clues the reader must gain an understanding into what Papa Bear is thinking.

I find this kind of writing dull except for the dialogue and would only use it for scripts. Even then, I want to give the reader more interesting cues and clues.

So did Shakespeare, for he wrote of one character in *A Winter's Tale*: "Exit, pursued by a bear." Probably Papa Bear.

So there they are, that quartet of possibilities: Omniscient, First Person, Limited Omniscient, Objective. But this knowledge is useful only up to a point. Knowing—and using—are two different problems.

Right at the beginning of a story, the author has a decision to make: What point of view will best serve the needs of the story?

Of course, what makes one book great—the quirky First-Person narration through a diary in *Catherine, Called Birdy* or in the straightforward bare-boned "I" voice of Karana in *Island of the Blue Dolphins*—may not work for another classic. I cannot imagine, for example, reading *Charlotte's Web* from Wilbur's little piggy self-centered point of view. Done that way, we would miss the opening section, which is Fern's story, and never hear her say, "Where is Papa going with that axe?" We would miss E.B. White's gorgeous prose poem extolling the beauties of a barn.

I have to tell you, though, that the choice an author makes can be altered as the book is being written. I remember working on the picture book *Honkers*, about a child whose mother is going through a bad pregnancy, so the girl is sent by train to stay with her grandparents. There she helps raise some geese (the Honkers of the title) from eggs. It is that little bit of mothering she herself does that gets her over the hump of homesickness and jealousy of the new baby.

When I first drafted *Honkers*, it was in First Person because I was modeling it on my very successful other bird book—*Owl Moon*. But my editor pointed out that the voice in *Honkers* was not as convincing, and then we sat down and tried to figure out why. When she suggested I try rewriting *Honkers* in third-person Limited Omniscient, all came clear.

I had not been able to enter into my young narrator's head in the direct way I had with the unnamed child in *Owl Moon*, because I was—in real life—more like the *Owl Moon* girl. The voice in that book had come out with ease. The "I" voice in *Honkers* eluded me. Going back—retreating, if you will—from the intimacy of the First Person to the objectivity of Third, allowed me to tell the story with a grace and power it had lacked in the first try.

Not so long ago, I wrote a YA novel, *Armageddon Summer*, with Bruce Coville, about a religious cult waiting atop a mountain in New England for the End of the World to arrive. We adopted alternating First-Person chapters from a girl and boy's point of view. This gave us a wonderfully intimate and up-close look at a religious cult from both a believer and a nonbeliever's point of view.

But about halfway through the book, we realized that there was a lot of information that our readers needed for a complete understanding of the story, information they were not getting and that we could not give them through our characters' eyes. To put it simply, there was no way these two teenagers would have had access to that information, but still we needed to impart it. So we adopted a Limited Omniscient stance for occasional interstitial chapters, such as an FBI report on the cult, the printout of a conversation between a policeman and his home base, two letters from the girl's mother to her husband who had refused to join the cult with them, and the like.

Sometimes in the matter of point of view, you need to be inventive.

Paul Fleischman has done this pushing of the point-of-view envelope quite successfully recently in his *Bull Run* book and in *Seedfolks*. But there is always the danger that the inventiveness can tip over into showboating. I always remember what Barry Moser once told me about typography. He called it *the invisible art*. "It only works when it does not call attention to itself," he warned. And point of view shifts should carry the same warning label.

As Henry Miller said about technique: "The best technique is no technique at all."

And Henry James, in a letter to Mrs. Humphrey Ward, said a similar thing. He was talking to her about a book she had shown him. He urged her to write from the consciousness of a particular character, saying: "Make that consciousness full, rich, universally prehensile, and stick to it—don't shift—and don't shift *arbitrarily*—how, otherwise, do you get your unity of subject or keep up your reader's sense of it?"

I want to remind you about another kind of narrative device, and that is the Unreliable Narrator. This is a narrator who sounds as if he is telling you the absolute truth but is not. And the only way a reader discovers the truth is to piece together clues along the way.

Often a First-Person narrator is unreliable. But, in fact, even the Omniscient narrator can be untruthful.

Back to the Three Bears to see how this can be so.

My neighbors, Mama Bear and Papa Bear, are the kindest folk in the forest. Loving, giving. Real salt-of-the-earth characters. Baby Bear's been raised the same way.

Anyone gets sick in the neighborhood, Mama Bear is the first one there with soup.

"Always do unto your neighbors," Papa Bear says every day to his son, "and they do you in turn." If I heard him once, I heard him a dozen times. It's something I take to heart, too, and teach my babies.

So when Goldilocks banged in their door, bunged up their rocker, binged on their porridge, and fell asleep without her pull-ups right there in the little one's bed, they had no choice really.

They ate her.

Suddenly what we thought the narrator was telling us and what we now know to be true are two different things.

Whichever way you look at the story, who you chose to be your narrator, whether the narrator is reliable—all these choices direct the story and guide the reader. The choice of narrator is perhaps the single most telling (pun intended) element of your story.

Whenever my children stand behind me crying, "author embellishment," they mean that I am changing the story and am not to be entirely believed. But when they tell the same stories, everything changes again. Different narrator, different tale.

We are all, when the matter is memory, unreliable narrators. Ask police about witnesses if you do not believe me.

After all, *Call me Ahab* can never be the same story as *Call me Ishmael*.

INTERLUDE
Never Turn Off the Writer's Head

I never turn off my writer's head.

Conversations are stuffed in there, the chalky sweet smell of paper-white roses, the sharp fishiness of herring fillets, the rough crumble of unharled stone, the way a pea plant points its wayward fingers upward in its search for some new purchase, how the ruined towers of a castle take on extra life against a gray sky, the feel of my granddaughter's small wriggly hand in mine. All this and more will be returned to me when I need it in a scene or a poem or as a central metaphor for a story.

I didn't know all that when I first began writing. I thought any time away from the typewriter was wasted time. I didn't understand the need to collect, to gather, to paste into the memory a variety of experiences.

Then my husband and I spent nine months camping in Europe and the Middle East, and this long years before computers. When we came back to the States, I found myself using images of what I had seen, tasted, touched, smelled, heard.

And my stories grew richer accordingly.

That's when I understood how important "gathering days" are for writers.

CHAPTER

Ay, now the plot thickens.

—GEORGE VILLIERS,
SECOND DUKE OF BUCKINGHAM;
THE REHEARSAL (111.11)

KILLING THE KING

Plot. What an odd word in the writer's vocabulary.

It signifies both what happens in story—and what does not.

It tokens cabals and machinations. Villains plot their evil, and then the plot takes an interesting or tragic turn. Plot goes forward and then doubles back on itself. It whirligigs, it dances, it climbs trees, it loves the wrong partner, it goes underground.

But plot can also point to setting, as in "this blessed plot, this earth, this realm, this England ..." in the large. And in the small, there is always a garden plot. And finally: one's cemetery plot.

However, in this chapter I want to attend to plot's usage for the novel writer because for most of us, the only place we will ever find a plot-driven life is in the pages of a book.

Let's look at plot and its several ways to make the story move. Note—I said: "move." I did not say "move forward." That is because sometimes plot moves us backward. And sometimes it moves us downward. And sometimes it moves us inward. And sometimes it reaches for the stars.

The most obvious characteristics of plot are: a beginning, a middle, an end. To write a book one need not reinvent plotting or set a precedent every time out. It can be that simple—beginning, middle, end.

But not so simple after all. The beginning must set the stage for something not as yet understood. It must begin the suspense. The middle will develop gradually, often in looping ways that would put a human's intestines to shame. And the end must be both surprising and inevitable. This is how I visualize a plot:

1. Beginning
2. Immediate consequences
3. The whirligig
4. Re-establishment
5. Whirligig again and again
6. Third whirligig, deepest emotional level
7. Denouement, inevitable and surprising

E.M. Forster has defined plot as "a narrative of events, the emphasis falling on causality." And he explains it this way: "'The king died and then the queen died,' is a story. 'The king died, and then the queen died of grief,' is a plot." He goes on to say that a story asks "And then?" but a plot asks "Why?"

But what Forster has given us is plot at its very minimum.

Let's try for a moment to take that sentence as the beginning of a plot and build from there. "The king died and then the queen died." Beginning with that opening sentence I can send the reader off in a thousand different directions.

First we have Forster's "The king died and then the queen died of grief."

But what if I added: "and a surfeit of bad mushrooms"?

Now we have the makings of a psychological drama. Did the queen poison herself, grief not being enough on its own? Or else we have a novel about a palace coup. Who—after all—prepared the mushrooms?

12

But what if, instead, I give the characters recognizable names? "Prince Albert died and the queen almost died of grief." We have a historical novel's plot in the making about Victoria. But if I said, "King Albert died and Queen Victoria died of grief," I have an alternate history novel's plot, for he was never actually king in name, and she actually lived and reigned for many years after.

What if I change only one word: The king died and the queen died of *laughter*.

Or add a phrase: The king died and the queen died of grief *forty years later*.

Or change the phrase: The king died and the queen died in prison. Or of boredom. Or a saint. Or before him.

Or using a pun: The king died and the queen dyed her hair.

As you can see, the permutations are quite literally (and literarily) endless. The putative plots start in exactly the same place, but go somewhere else each time.

Besides—Forster's "The king died" definition is too simple for us these days, some seventy years after his groundbreaking book, *Aspects of the Novel*. We have in that time invented, among other things, the plotless novel, the novel that goes back to front, and the novel that is all plot without anything else.

A textbook definition of plot would be: the sequence of narrative order. Or: the sequence of events showing characters in action.

Anthony Trollope sees plot as a "contrived arrangement of incidents by which interest is excited."

W. Somerset Maugham sees it as "... a line to direct the reader's interest. That is quite possibly the most important thing in fiction, for it is by the direction of interest that the author carries the reader along from page to page ..."

And British children's book writer Elizabeth Hawkins says: "It's rather unfashionable to talk of plotting in literary circles these days. It's too often associated with down market, five hundred page blockbusters, which, if true, are often examples of skilled plotting. How else would you last through five hundred pages?"

But in fact, when thinking about plot, it is best to remember what some British school children said when asked what writers they liked to read. The answer was Enid Blyton, because "there's always something going on."

Always something going on.

In some ways plot boils down to those four words.

Always something going on.

It is the writer's privilege, really, to order events, to plan sequence, to focus on one strand of an existence while ignoring all others. We cannot do this in reality—but we can on the pages of a book.

So here's my plot.

The king died, and the queen went into the woods to think about life without him and about her own popularity, as opposed to her stepson, the new king, with his nasty propensity for cruelty. There she is attacked by giant squid, who took her below the water where she teaches them the fundamentals of good hygiene and they teach her the salubrious effects of democracy. She falls in love with the largest squid, a handsome fellow with the tenderest of tentacles, but gives him up because her country needs her more. She returns to the waterless realm where, as queen mother, she is given a grand banquet where she is served surf-and-turf. On that platter, surrounded by bad mushrooms, is a plate of giant calamari. She recognizes the tentacles as being those that had so recently caressed her. She realizes, also, that the mushrooms are amanita and that the new king, her stepson—angry at her return because she is popular with the people—wants her to die, and die horribly in front of him. Deliberately she eats the mushrooms and, with the words "Power to the people" on her lips, falls atop her erstwhile eight-armed lover. It is the signal for revolution.

There you have it—always something going on.

A plot. Written in five minutes.

And silly as it is, it does have all the elements a plot should have.

1. BEGINNING

The king dies.

Now, when you actually come to write the story, this deathbed scene could be broadly played, with courtiers gathered around the chamber and much weeping and wailing and gnashing of teeth. Or it could be set in the middle of a battle, an uprising perhaps, the king's awful son by his side, with the two of them trading blows with the enemy and retorts with one another. Or in the garden among the roses, or on the battlements with the king's soldiers by his side, or on the potty, his royal trousers down around his knees.

However the story accomplishes the king's death, all the plot outline says to us right now is—*the king dies*. Dies horribly or nobly or tragically or humorously. But he dies.

2. THE IMMEDIATE CONSEQUENCES

The queen goes outside to grieve.

She also goes outside to think not just about her grief, which gives us our *core emotion*, which is also another way of saying *conflict*, but to think, too, about the secondary emotions—her connection with the country and her relationship with her stepson. This is much broader and wider thematically and—as you can see from what else happens—it is actually more important than (or at least equally important as) her grief.

As writers, we are often reminded about theme. Some people mistake theme for plot. Theme is an overarching idea that encompasses the entire story. Or underlies it like a basement. (See chapter seven, "Building the House.") Plot is what is moving along one foot after another, often fueled by the theme, sometimes following the theme like a magus after a star.

The larger the novel, the more important it is to have more than one core emotion, more than one conflict. In life we work simultaneously on many emotions; we are in fact often broken on the rack of conflicting desires and needs. We stew in an emotional pot. (I know it feels like only teenagers do this, but be reasonable. We are all teens grown old.)

Life, however, is not art. Art is a lot tidier. Ivy Compton-Burnett has written, "Real life seems to have no plots.

And as I think a plot desirable and almost necessary I have this extra grudge against life."

3. THE WHIRLIGIG

(We up the ante. We give the plot a ratcheting twist.)

The queen is kidnapped.

Well, obviously *something* had to happen. We couldn't just leave her weeping all alone in the garden. Weeping and thinking. That would be boring. Life may be boring, which is why Ivy Compton-Burnett bears it a grudge. But in art, boring is bad. As Isaac Bashevis Singer once said, "Truth in art that is boring is not true."

Something big must happen. Something major must go on to make a novel readable and interesting. There is no plot if the queen just sits in the orchard on a garden seat and weeps, not even if she then goes into the woods and thinks deep thoughts. We would soon tire of her and pick up instead one of those blockbuster page-turners.

The author must move the queen out into the action. Bad move perhaps in chess, necessary in the novel.

This is what we call thickening the plot. From George Villiers, Second Duke of Buckingham: "Ay, now the plot thickens very much upon us." (And I bet you thought it was Shakespeare.)

Intense action is what happens when the plot gets thickened like a fine stew. The king dying is one action, an opening. The queen going out to grieve is another action. But these are small scratches of the pen on an otherwise blank page. Now is the time for something to be writ large on that page. Kidnapping is large!

Now, it needn't be kidnapping, of course. A good plot needs conflict, but it can be a protagonist (our main character) struggling against another person (an antagonist), or against self (see Le Guin's *A Wizard of Earthsea* where Ged struggles against his darker side), or against society (*Charlotte's Web*, where Wilbur's struggle is with a world that eats pigs), or even a struggle against nature (Daniel Defoe's *Robinson Crusoe*, Scott O'Dell's *Island of the Blue Dolphins*, Jean Craighead George's *My Side of the Mountain* and *Julie of the Wolves*, and everything Gary Paulsen ever wrote).

But in this case I have chosen kidnappers. And giant squid is certainly surprising. (Surprising-funny is not necessarily surprising-good.) The kidnappers needn't actually be squid. They could be aardvarks or centaurs or the blue-painted Picts. They could be the local democrats. Or the Taliban. They could be a band of marauding Amazons.

They just need to be The Other.

Though if you could pull off giant squid simply by the power of your writing, you could be the next Terry Pratchett or Roald Dahl or J.K. Rowling or Ursula K. Le Guin.

Actually, I like to be as surprised as my readers. The queen is in the orchard keening and then … wait for it. Something moves in.

This happened once when I was working on a fantasy novel, *White Jenna*, the second book in a fantasy trilogy. A bunch of rowdy green-skinned elves suddenly appeared to confront my hero, Jenna.

"No!" I told them. "Go away! This is not an elf novel!"

But they set up tents, started a campfire, refused to move.

In a huff I put the book aside. One week. Two. I went on strike and did not write a word more.

On the third week of passive resistance, I gave in.

"Why are you here?" I asked them.

They told me—and they were right. They solved an important plot problem, a time problem, and an emotional problem, all in one sweep. And also explained something I had neglected to explain in the first book, *Sister Light, Sister Dark*.

So if elves—or the giant squid—march into your plot, at least hear them out. They may be just the movement you need.

4. RE-ESTABLISH

(Having upped the ante, we need to bring it to a new level playing field, a kind of new beginning, which is really a middle passage.)

The Kingdom Under the Sea.

Now the reader is truly hooked. You have set up all your patterns of conflict and antagonism. Having got the reader's attention, you now have time to do something interesting.

The Kingdom Under the Sea, in the plot, is the place of the re-establishing moment. We are seeing the kingdom, of course, through the eyes of our queen. But once her initial fear is over, she can assess and process and any other -*cess* you wish.

And the reader—along with the main character—can take a moment to enjoy this new place. (Or conversely, can take a moment to really hate the place if this is a fear setting.) Anyway, after the first whirligig, the reader, like the queen, needs a place to rest.

Now, as an aside—some plots are really a series of episodes or set pieces strung together, little saltwater pearls on a strand, lovely though not entirely matched. *Alice's Adventures in Wonderland*, for example. *Stuart Little. The Phantom Tollbooth. Gulliver's Travels. Tom Jones.* Do not expect the same kind of ratcheting whirligig and re-establishment to go on with those books. I am talking about the more ordinary novel. (Besides, genius first defines and then defies rules. I am not a genius. I expect few of you are either.)

The time of re-establishment is not only where we get our second breath in the novel, it is also the time that we can underline the central core emotions and get a new look at that theme (which may have been as difficult to spot earlier as a spring warbler in a thick copse of trees). It may also introduce us to important secondary characters.

5. WHIRLIGIG AGAIN AND AGAIN

(After that much-needed rest, we can go on. Time to give the whirligig another turn.)

The queen teaches the squid something and learns something interesting herself.

5 1/2. ANOTHER MORE IMPORTANT TWIST OF THE TALE

The queen falls in love with the largest squid, a handsome fellow with the tenderest of tentacles.

George Meredith wrote:

> In tragic life, God wot,
> No villain need be! Passions spin the plot;
> We are betrayed by what is false within.

Passions spinning the plot indeed. That is what must come now. No more deaths for a moment, not another kidnapping. Now we must work with something more difficult—the wealth of passions we have uncovered. For it turns out that the one we thought our antagonist is really not. (The old Gothic shift—the dark saturnine man is really the good guy, the bright-eyed blonde is shifty.)

What we have done with these two twists, of course, is to double back on the queen's early grief and her presumed love for the king.

Think of it. The first scene with the king dying may now have to be reassessed. Maybe the young prince comes by his villainous tendencies legitimately. Maybe this was a forced marriage. If the queen can so easily fall in love with a squid, or an alien, or a peasant rebel, or another woman, or ... whomever ... what does that tell us about her? About her previous relationship with the king? With the kingdom? With the stepson?

The plot has now reached the time when it must deal with all these emotions. The reader must be forced to think again and re-evaluate those opening bits.

Hey—maybe the queen is a giant squid herself!

A good plot does not just look forward. It forces us backward and sideward as well. It makes us look inward as well as outward. Think of plot as a kind of time-travel device. While it goes ahead, it changes what it has passed through; it rearranges where it has been.

6. THIRD WHIRLIGIG

(The deepest emotional level: now the penultimate twist. The whirligig spins around again.)

The queen gives up her lover because her country needs her more.

Now we see what kind of character the queen really has. She has been tested, not just with the king's death. She has now been tested in the deeper cauldron of the soul, where the plot has been heading all along. This recasts the story once again: What she does now is to become a sun that makes the king and prince and giant squid lover cast different shadows. We are blinded by that sun, then warmed by it. We read the book anew by its light.

This is what I mean by a plot not just looking forward. If it simply looked forward, the twists would need to be straightened out, the characters would lose depth. The plot needs to shadow and foreshadow and backshadow as well.

7. DENOUEMENT

(The ending that is both inevitable and surprising.)

The queen's return and death and transfiguration.

Here we can ring as many changes as we want, a whole series of small whirlpools that create an incredible undertow of emotion and satisfaction: The queen comes back and we see how she is greeted—by the prince, by those in power, by those not in power. We think all is well.

But all is not well.

A plot should hold the best surprise until last, of course. By this I do not mean that every story needs a punch line. Anecdotes and jokes have punch lines that often confound all that has gone before. A story's ending must be a surprise but a satisfying one, an organic whole.

The queen is given a feast.

Perhaps we readers have forgotten the prince's proclivities toward cruelty. Or ignored them. Boys will be boys and princes will be princes. Perhaps we did not see those proclivities as more than an irrational tic. But now we understand. And the queen understands, too. The prince/now king serves her a meal of her lover. The squid's tentacles, or the head of the peasant, or the breast of her Amazon partner. It does not matter which. If the queen is the sun, the prince is the moon. The shadows he makes the others throw are of a different nature altogether.

We think we know the ending, but still we do not know. We are watching the eddies; we miss the undertow.

The queen makes a final choice. It is a choice for love. For freedom. For history. It surprises us. But if we had been paying careful attention, it should not surprise us. Hadn't she gone into the garden to think, musing upon her country? Hadn't she learned about democracy in the Kingdom Under the Sea? Hadn't she fallen in love and chosen duty over passion? On rereading the plot, we realize that ending had been coming, inevitably, all along.

Or as is said in Shakespeare's *Henry IV*: "A good plot, good friends, and full of expectation."

Do not take my seven stages of plotting as gospel.

Never take any writing teacher's advice as gospel.

Each author is different. Each book is different. Each demands a different counting. For me what seems important are: beginning, middle, and end, and some surprising twists along the way. But you may have a different narrative movement in mind.

Some writers plot a thing in minute detail before going on with the book. Some know where the book will end before they start. Me, I like to set the characters in motion with: "The king died and ..." I find out where the queen is going as she herself finds out. Hand in hand on the same adventure.

Writing *Armageddon Summer* with Bruce Coville was an interesting adventure. He is a writer who wants to know his plot before beginning. Like my husband, he reads maps. I, on the other hand, prefer letting the plot grow out of the characters, following their lead.

Which one of us is right?

Let's just say we had ... creative differences.

How did it come out? Stubborn is as stubborn does. Bruce kept saying, "Shouldn't we sit down and talk about the plot?" And I kept saying, "Soon. Very soon." And when we got to within the last four chapters, I said, "Now we can plot this sucker."

And we did.

Chekhov once commented: "I think when one has finished writing a short story one should delete the beginning and the end." This method led John Galsworthy to comment about Chekhov's stories that they were "all middle, like a tortoise."

I don't believe that most readers like tortoise stories. But I also don't believe that you should write for the dictates of an unknowable audience. You should listen to the story and the steady rhythm of your own writer's heart.

I think really the best to be said about plot is: *Always something going on.*

Sometimes going on forward. Sometimes backward. Sometimes like the great snake Ouroboros with its tail in its mouth—that gnostic symbol of infinity—just going on.

❧ ❧ ❧
INTERLUDE
Worrying About Depth

I always worry about *depth* when I'm writing novels —
where to put it in and how.

One of my online discussion groups was wrestling
with this very problem. Someone's editor had told her
she had to add depth to her book.

One teaspoon, stir vigorously, I suppose.

The editor used an onion metaphor.

I responded: "Every time an editor wants to talk about
plots and depth, they bring in the old onion. Honestly, I
am tired of that onion and think editors should retire it
as an overdone metaphor. Maybe we should send them
a rejection letter …"

One of my friends answered back with this hilarious bit:

Dear Editor:

While your metaphor is well told and has some merit, I'm
afraid it's not right for me at this time. The premise is a
little overworked, and I have recently acquired a similar
metaphor from another editor.

Other writers may feel differently, however, and I wish
you luck placing this metaphor elsewhere.

I would, however, be willing to listen to any analogies
you might make in the future.

Sincerely,
I.B. Weary

CHAPTER

The ultimate concern of the artist is not
to paint mountains and clouds and trees
but the air between them.

—WANG WEI

AN ERUPTION
OF POPPIES

Too many writers ignore landscape, to their peril. Perhaps the problem is their lack of visual acuity. We are unpracticed in the art of looking.

Nobody has taught us to see. Except in art courses, we are never told the value of looking at what is all around us. Oh, if something big moves—a bear, a truck, a train, a moose—we will notice. And get out of the way. But most of us miss the little things or the immovable objects. Or if we notice, it is a fleeting moment, then gone.

For the majority of people, landscape is simply just there. It exerts no gravitational pull on our senses. We walk through it, slap at it, step over it, break off a piece. But observe it carefully? That takes too long.

Many authors know this about landscape: that it is the setting or background for their characters. But the better authors realize much more. Place can be shorthand (or longhand) to explain a hero or villain: Think of the difference between the living green forest of Ents and the Orc-made desert of Mordor in *The Lord of the Rings*.

Better writers also know that landscape can be metaphor, can be a parallel to their characters' lives, can become central to the action, can even be a character in itself.

Think of R.L. Stevenson's Davie Balfour, striding across the harsh Highland countryside, becoming a man. The territory he treads helps shape him.

(13)

Think of the uncompromising sea through which Captain Ahab plows and how it defines him, creates him just as the whale Moby Dick "tasks" him and "heaps" him.

Or how the rough island on which Robinson Crusoe is marooned is the making of his soul.

How Mary Lennox is changed by her secret garden, how she blossoms and grows strong within its stone walls.

Think of the cozy familiarity of the March girls' landscape, how the careful plantings, the warm comfortable house, emphasizes their domesticity as they grow from little women into mature ones. Then consider Catherine Earnshaw and Heathcliff, as wild and untamable as their windswept moors.

Sometimes, as in the *Dune* books, the arid desert through which the sand worms tunnel becomes a metaphor for the life lived. Sometimes, as in the island on which Ratty and Mole find the living Pan in *The Wind in the Willows*, landscape is the beating heart of the book. And just see what the variety of landscapes do to poor Gulliver in his travels or Alice in her Wonderland.

In the stories written about King Arthur there are many characters: Arthur, who is the king despite himself, valorous and trusting and true. Merlin, the magic maker, who unmakes himself through love. Guinevere, married to a king, loved by a knight, trying to remain true to both and to herself as well. Lancelot, the perfect knight, whose perfection is a trap for all. And the others: Morgan le Fey, Mordred, Bors, Gawaine, the Green Knight, the Lady of the Lake, Elaine … characters who live on and on. But the character that interests me the most is Camelot itself.

Whether it is a place of turrets and ballrooms shining on a hill, or a rough turf-and-timbered fortress surrounded by a stone shell wall; whether we call it Camelot or Camlann or something else entirely, that castle focuses our attention. It tells us that within this place magic, mystery, adventure, and romance will happen. It is a spot that is both within time and without.

So when I wrote my YA novel about King Arthur— *Sword of the Rightful King*—the castle became a character on its own.

However, it's not just Arthurian stories that demand that kind of landscape. All novels work best when they have a landscape that seems real, alive, purposeful, important.

Philippa Pearce writes in her lovely fantasy novel for children, *Tom's Midnight Garden*, "There is a time, between night and day, when landscapes sleep." It is a lovely line, full of the promise of magic. And magic is what happens. Tom goes through the back door of the flat, though he's been told it leads only to an alley strewn with garbage cans. And there, magically, a garden appears, a Victorian garden from the 1880s, with broad sweeps of lawn and yew hedges, and a water tank filled with the flash of goldfish.

Pearce's description of the garden echoes her own love of landscape, and her words truly are magical:

> At first [Tom] took the outermost paths, gravelled and box-edged, intending to map for himself their farthest extent. Then he broke away impatiently on a cross-path. It tunneled through the gloom of yew-trees arching overhead from one side, and hazelnut stubs from the other: Ahead

was a grey-green triangle of light where the path must
come out into the open again. Underfoot the earth was
soft with the humus of last year's rotted leaves ...

and a few sentences later ...

His path came out by the asparagus beds of the kitchen-
garden—so he found them later to be. Beyond their long,
grave-like mounds was a dark oblong—a pond. At one
end of the pond, and overlooking it, stood an octagonal
summer-house with an arcaded base and stone steps up
to its door. The summer-house, like the rest of the garden,
was asleep on its feet.

Already the reader is as enchanted as Tom. But the description of the garden—walled on three sides, a lawn, a fir
tree wound with ivy, a hedge with a hole in it just the
size for a boy to squeeze through, then a meadow with
cows, and geese in the long grasses—the description
goes on for another three pages.

Just so lovingly, Robin McKinley describes the Beast's
garden in *Beauty*. A keen gardener herself, McKinley's
visual sense of the garden is word perfect.

She writes:

Beauty's father was distracted from his pleasant musings
by a walled garden opening off the path to his right; the
wall was waist-high, and covered with the largest and most
beautiful climbing roses that he had ever seen. The garden
was full of them; inside the rose-covered wall were rows of
bushes: white roses, red roses, yellow, pink, flame-colour,
maroon; and a red so dark it was almost black.

This arbor of roses seemed somehow different from the great gardens that lay all around the castle, but different in some fashion he could not define. The castle and its gardens were everywhere silent and beautifully kept; but there was a self-containment, even almost a self-aware-ness here, that was reflected in the petals of each and every rose, and drew his eyes from the path.

He dismounted and walked in through a gap in the wall, the reins in his hand; the smell of these flowers was wilder and sweeter than that of poppies. The ground was carpeted with petals, and yet none of the flowers were dead or dying; they ranged from buds to the fullest bloom, but all were fresh and lovely. The petals he and the horse trampled underfoot took no bruise.

In Alice Hoffman's *The Probable Future*, the Sparrow family of magical women are all intimate with the landscape. Hoffman, too, knows such things, describing spring this way:

... the smell of the laurel, so spicy just before blooming, the way everything turned green, all at once, as though winter itself were a dream, a fleeting nightmare made up of ice and heartlessness and sorrow.

As well as this:

... the yearly flight of returning cowbirds and blackbirds and sparrows, flocks whose great numbers blocked out the sun for an entire day every year, a winged and breathing eclipse of the pale, untrustworthy sky.

The generous literary landscape—whether garden or mountainside, forest or copse, moor or plain—is as much a part of these stories as the plot, the characters, the theme.

Still, the problem comes down to this: how to visualize a landscape well enough that the reader is truly there? I can take a friend by the hand and lead him around my garden in Massachusetts or along the St. Andrews coastline in Fife. But how does a writer lead a reader?

Perhaps it would be helpful to think of landscape as coming in three parts.

First, find the large shapes. Some are immovable and, in human terms, immutable. Ask yourself how the mountains are defined against the sky. Are they so far away they are fuzzy and muzzy around the edges? Are they lumpy, which makes them older, or sharp and pointed, which means they are younger and have not yet been worn away? Read some good books on geology and construct your mountain ranges accordingly, because a mountain landscape made by volcanic action will be different from one that has been carved out by eons of rivers meandering down their sides.

Water—rivers, streams, oceans—certainly moves within its banks and sometimes in fierce storms or in the aftermath of runoffs even breaks over those banks. How to describe them so the reader actually sees the shifting blues and greens, the foaming spume of white water, the tumble of waves? What about the shadows of fingerlings darting along the sandy bottoms, or the whale that humps out of the blue-black water?

Some large shapes are mobile and shifting. What about the clouds? Are they streamers or plump cumulus?

Are they white as ibis feathers or gray as stone? (And by the way, do you see a difference in the colors gray and grey?)

Do the trees rise up like fists or spread out like fingers? Does the mountain wear a stubble of small trees on its face?

With such depictions of landscape, the writer can set a mood, background music for the eye. Or can set up the landscape to act contrapuntally against (or with) the hero.

Second, there are singular features: a rock, flower, vine, bird against the slate of sky. These individuals are punctuations of landscape, used instead of an exclamation point.

Perhaps you could place a solitary gnarled tree to stand defiantly upon a hill. Or place a blood-colored flower near the outstretched hand of a dead knight. As your hero treads up a hill, heedless of the pine needles underfoot or the wuthering of the wind tangling her hair, the reader sees the character in motion. By watching his actions on the landscape or in concert with it, the reader does not need to be told how he is feeling. Editor Patricia Gauch calls it "floating" when a character seems to be disconnected or unconnected with the landscape. "Where is he?" she asks her authors. "How strong is the wind? How hot is the sun? What color are the rocks? Do the shadows tell us the time of day?"

Third, know that landscape well enough to individualize the features: gray porous rock, spikes of yew, eruptions of red poppies in a green field, blue morning glories straining for the sun, a hawk in a perilous stoop taking its living from the sky.

Go outside and walk about. Don't take notes, but let yourself truly see what is in front of you, above you, below you. Sit still for a half-hour, for an hour, and watch what goes on around you. Life happens. Busy, mobile life. If you do not move, you will not affect it. You will be an eye only. A careful, studious, sometimes startled eye.

What might you see? Ants and beetles scurrying by your boots, a woodpecker flecking the bark behind you, a squirrel stopping to gaze at you with its black button eyes, a butterfly resting on your shoulder with a tremor of wings.

If you are luckier, a rabbit will skitter by your feet, a fox with its flagged tail will stalk by, a deer might find its way to a stream and stand drinking with its long tongue, a flash of trout might ripple the water.

In the city, though the buildings take the place of the large shapes of mountains, there is still a great deal to see: birds, beetles, green shoots springing up through the cracks in the pavement, wallflowers perching precariously atop stone abutments, gargoyles that wink in the rain, the changing shape of shadows gray on gray.

The trick is that the details of the landscape must be precise. It is as if the author has been there, not just a visitor but a native of the place.

Henry James said about the novel that its supreme virtue is its "solidity of specification." And award-winning children's book author Lloyd Alexander echoes this when talking about his own novels. "What appears gossamer is underneath as solid as pre-stressed concrete."

Some authors get to that specificity by making lists, writing out travelogues, drawing maps, researching seasons/flora/fauna in books. But first of all, the author must become an observer: of nature as well as of character.

If you do not look, you cannot see. If you cannot see, how can you write well enough to make others see? How can you write well enough to keep your characters from floating?

And after you see, you must learn to hear: unseen frogs chorusing in the fading light, the weeping cry of a screech owl, the long fall of a coyote's voice.

And after that the smells: the sharp brine of ocean, the pong of rotting seaweed, the crisp mountain air scented lightly with pine.

And how—I hear you ask—to keep all of this in your head? You don't, unless you are a wildlife expert, a rare gardener, a butterfly fancier as fine as Nabokov, a fly fisherman extraordinaire, or live (as I do) with a birding expert. Actually, none of us can keep it all in our heads. I bet even Peter Matthiessen has to do his homework.

So, on your research shelves, close at hand, you will store bird books and mushroom identification books, books about animal tracks and seashells and the changing face of forests. Buy secondhand Audubon guides, and when you go on vacation bring home all the pamphlets you can find. These go right next to your thesaurus and dictionary and books of timelines and rhyming dictionary and encyclopedias and The Elements of Style.

13

But first and most important, go outside. Sit in a shadow. Become part of the tree. Watch the world. Drink it in.

And then write it. All of it. As much as you can get down. Landscape as character, as metaphor, as background and foreground, as counterpoint to your hero, as villain, as friend. Become that better writer who knows the worth of landscape and can set down what is seen to illuminate what is not seen. Draw that world with your words, and you will draw the readers in.

∢ ❢ ∢

INTERLUDE
Trust the Hindbrain

I don't force my writing, I let things grow organically.

I trust the hindbrain to work at a problem even when the forebrain is engaged in other activities.

Samuel Johnson said, "What is written without effort is in general read without pleasure."

But how do we count effort? Is it simply sitting down and working every day without fail?

Is it following a thread of plot till the end?

Is it allowing the imagination to range over a variety of projects?

Is it trusting the hindbrain to solve what seems unsolvable?

I contend that a writer is always working, whether standing or sitting, whether lying down in a hot bath or walking up a steep hill, whether brainstorming with an editor or dreaming on a train trip.

Activity that stimulates the cardiovascular system also stimulates the imagination.

Don't forget to smell the grandbabies.

Pay attention to good food.

Lie down on your stomach in the tall grass.

Listen to the rhythm of ocean waves.

Put your hand on graven stone. Finger silk. Touch a loved one's hair.

Breathe in the world.

CHAPTER

Writers live twice.

—NATALIE GOLDBERG

OUT WITH OUTLINES

Not all books can be outlined successfully. If they could, we wouldn't need to write the books. Or read them. One must remember that the map is not the territory. All plans for writing must be revisable.

Outlines know everything about a book and nothing about the story. Story is organic, and it is better to encourage it to grow toward the light.

Look at these mini-encapsulations of famous books. See if you can get the real flavor of the book from reading these. Think of what you are missing.

I call them Crushed Classics.

Or perhaps Rushed Readings.

ANNA KARENINA

Anna was a good woman.

She met a bad man.

She met a fast train.

Whooooooo. Whooooooo.

Thud.

The End.

THE SCARLET LETTER

Hester Prynne was a bad girl.

Still she got an A.

JANE EYRE

Mr. Rochester had a bad wife

And a good wife.

One set fires.

One ran for her life.

Run, Jane, run.

HAMLET

A new kind of hero:

Danish ham on wry.

MACBETH, ONE

Mr. Macbeth and Mrs. Macbeth

Got their hands dirty.

Out, spot, out.

MACBETH, TWO

A Scottish lady

Had a Big Mac attack.

MACBETH, THREE

Between the witch

And the bitch,

Macbeth gets treed.

THE LORD OF THE RINGS

Yo!

Fro!

Give the mountain the finger!

THE LAST DAYS OF POMPEII

BOOM!

That's the sound

of all the people in Pompeii

making ashes of themselves.

THE ADVENTURES OF HUCKLEBERRY FINN

Rift-raft

on the Big Muddy.

ANIMAL FARM, ONE

From baaaaaaaaad

To worse.

ANIMAL FARM, TWO

Where is the big bad wolf

When you really need him?

ANIMAL FARM, THREE

A boaring book,

or how to make a real pig of yourself

Without really trying.

ETHAN FROME

A man with

A sliding scale of values

Should never marry

In New England.

OTHELLO

No Moor

Hanky-panky.

MOBY-DICK, ONE

Ahab's aim

Didn't suck.

Moby Dick

Didn't duck.

Bad timing.

14

Worse luck.

For both of them.

MOBY-DICK, TWO

Call me Fishmeal.

MOBY-DICK, THREE

See the white whale.

See the big tail.

Row, Ish, row.

THE TAMING OF THE SHREW

Kate-r-wauling

leads to brawling,

and a mauling.

A feminist Kate-tastrophe.

Amusing? I hope so. But they tell us as little about a book as an outline would. What makes a book is not the outline, the theme, the idea, the characters. It is the gestalt. All of everything together.

Moviemakers at pitch meetings like to be able to tell the story in a referential manner, with a single line or two at most. *Romeo and Juliet meet Mr. Ed. Santa riding National Velvet. The Lost Girls go out on strike against Peter Pan.* But the real movies take time. And even more so do books.

An outline (or a find-out-line, as I used to call it) can be a straitjacket for some, a straight path for others. Just don't expect it to do all of your work.

❦

INTERLUDE
The Difference Between Writer and Reader

How different writing a book is from reading one. When you read a book, no matter how much you are engrossed between the covers, when you get to the last page, you will most likely put it away and pick up a new book to read.

However, the writer is stuck in that same book for days and weeks and months and sometimes years. We live inside the book differently than our readers, even our most obsessive readers. We walk the land, shadowing our heroes. We are the first to taste the poisoned draught. We feel the knife's blade go in. We weep, we laugh, we feel the north wind like a slap against the face. We take out the poison and put in a sleeping potion. We change the knife to a sword. The north wind circles around to the east. We feel it all again.

So when you are writing, better be certain that particular novel is a place you want to be. You are going to take up residence there for quite some time.

CHAPTER

When I'm really writing,
I'm listening.

—MADELEINE L'ENGLE

THE ALPHABETICS
OF WRITING

A IS FOR ARMATURE, that thing that goes under a statue. No, not the piece it rests on, but the skeleton, the structure, the shining bones.

It is up to the writer to so well clothe those bones that nothing pokes through. Any book with bones sticking out awkwardly through the skin needs an ambulance (another A word). And a book that needs such resuscitation is a failure.

B IS FOR BOTOX, the wrinkle cure based on a deadly poison. Women of a certain age (and a certain class) seem to feel a need to inject Botox into their foreheads to make them look younger, or at least smoother. But I believe wrinkles are far more interesting than a tabula rasa. This may be because I grew up in Manhattan and New England where the horizontals are broken up with strong verticals, whether skyscrapers or mountain ranges. The flatland does not appeal to me. Nor does the flat forehead, except for the wonderful ready smoothness of a child's. However, in fiction, wrinkles are imperative. Otherwise there is a blandness, a Stepford syndrome where all the characters seem the same. So writers should cultivate wrinkles, not Botox.

C IS FOR COLLABORATION, though not quite in the way you may think. Of course, comic books, picture books, and plays are all immediately recognizable as collaborations—between author and artist, author and actors. But every genre of writing is a collaboration—between author and editor, and then between author and reader. Besides, what is an editor if not an educated and critical first reader? So a writer who denies or refuses the idea of collaboration is fooling himself. Listen to the editor, use that reader's comments to help you restructure, rework, and rewrite. The editor may not know *how* to fix something but will be good at giving you a signal that there is a problem. Fixing that problem is up to you.

C IS ALSO FOR COAL. I love the compressed universes of poetry (pun intended). Poetry is making coal into diamonds but never forgetting the dark power of the coal.

D IS FOR DESSERT and the button I have had for years that reads, "Life is uncertain, eat dessert first." Which part of your literary meal do you start with? Some authors begin at the beginning, some in the middle, some with character lists, some with plot points, some with research. And they are all correct! I knew one author who always had to stick the title "You Can't Go Home Again" at the top of her page before sitting down to write. That title never lasted, of course, but it was her way of beginning. I always need a title as well, but it varies according to the piece. Another writer friend has to know the ending of her story before she can begin. "Otherwise," she told me, "I am sailing off into the unknown without a rudder or map." I actually love sailing that way. It makes the uncertain trip as exciting for me as for any reader. And we can eat chocolate along the way.

E IS FOR EGGS, which are perfect for some and deadly poison for others. My husband starts every morning with two or three poached eggs. (And no, dear reader, he cooks them himself!) My friend Walter is so allergic to eggs that even an eggless meal cooked in a pan that has recently seen an egg across a crowded kitchen can be deadly to him. (You should hear his wife ordering at a restaurant!) Often I hear of teachers who insist on egg books for everyone in the class, as though enough exposure could defeat any allergy. The same goes for writers. If you cannot even bear to read horror novels, or romance novels, or westerns, or stream-of-consciousness novels, or slim books of poetry, don't suddenly try and write them. You are allergic. Accept that. Move on.

F IS FOR FURBELOW, one of those words I have always loved and wanted to put in a story. Ditto the following words: pentimento, taradiddle, Sargasso, *taghairm*, fewmets, frass. But words are the building blocks of stories, not the reason for them. Wait—I did use fewmets early and often in my Pit Dragon series. So sometimes, if you hang around words long enough, you will find a place for them. And if you do not know my words, look them up! (Though you will have to find *taghairm* in a Scottish or Celtic dictionary. It means "to prophesy while wrapped in a bullock's skin behind a waterfall." Not something one can slip into a story easily.)

G IS FOR GRADUATION, which is what every publication day feels like when you can hold up the magazine, journal, broadside, or book and find your name under the title. That published work is a certification of a course taken. Grade A-plus. Summa cum laude. A sign to the outside world that one is now an adult, a grown-up writer, with the paper to prove it. The difficult thing for writers to cope with, though, is that every single new piece of writing is another course, and not all courses lead to graduation. I used to think that once I was published it was all smooth sailing after that: no more rejections (hah!), no more editorial revision letters (haha!) no more money worries (hahaha!). I also thought that once I had learned how to write number one, a poem; number two, a short story; number three, a picture book; number four, a novel, I would be able to apply this knowledge forever to my writing. But each new piece of writing is a learning experience. Truly, such schooling goes on forever.

H IS FOR HOPEFUL, NOT HAPPY, ENDINGS. No one outside a fairy tale should expect a happy ending. We can all be happy for an hour or two. Someone who is consistently happy forever has simply not looked through her neighbor's curtains. A happy ending means the story stops, right there, at the last word. A hopeful ending promises more. And what satisfied reader doesn't want more? Think about it—what if Cinderella and her prince pledged to make one another happy "for richer and for poorer." Only one of them knows the difference. As author Nalo Hopkinson has written: "I like my endings to have many notes; something lost, something learned, something regretted, something salvaged, something gained." Tough magic demands tough sacrifice—or at least the willingness for sacrifice. The good writer doesn't just put the ram on the rock in Isaac's place. The reader needs to know what Jacob and Isaac have both gotten from the experience. The story should not just shout: "King's X." In a meaningful ending there must be a lifetime of discussion, accusations, recriminations, understanding, wrestling with angels.

H IS ALSO FOR "HIGH CONCEPT," an idea publishers have borrowed from movie producers. High concept means an easily understood three- or four-word description that POPS!

Romeo and Juliet, only one is a robot.
Alice's Adventures in Wonderland pop-up book.
Madonna writes a children's book.
Captain Ahab fights a Great White Alien.
Dick and Jane in Wonderland.
The Last Voyage of Reepicheep.
Beauty and the Beast where they are both gay boys.
Sleeping Beauty's prince kisses the scullery maid.
Madonna writes another children's book.

I IS FOR IGLOO, an uncomfortable place for most of us to live. To live within the pages of most books would be just as uncomfortable. The hairbreadth escapes, the wounds (both physical and emotional), the outbursts and inbursts alone would paralyze most of us. Imagine tracking Jean Valjean through the Paris sewers or following Inspector Rebus into the dark streets of Edinburgh after a murderer. Imagine sailing on a raft down the muddy Mississippi with an escaped slave as a companion. Or standing back-to-back with Lt. Sharpe and the Forlorn

Hope while fighting off Napoleon's finest. Imagine racing around the world in eighty days in a balloon, or facing down an enraged witch with only a pail of water. In real life most of us would suffer fatal heart attacks or come out of the adventures with the shingles or at least needing a long course with a psychiatrist. Plus wanting a long, hot bath and plenty of good soap. Books are, of course, a place of borrowed courage. But to live there? Not on your life.

J IS FOR JUNCO HYEMALIS, a lovely little gray-and-white bird that frequents our feeders. I love this unassuming bird with its gray head and breast, white belly, and white outer tail feathers. It's not as majestic as the eagles that soar nearby, or as haunting as the great horned owls, or startling as the red splotch of the cardinal, or as jaunty as the flashy blue jay. But I love the junco, which we in New England call "snowbird" because he always seems to be there in the winter to lighten the dark days. Just so I love small poems that might get passed by, or short fiction. I love to read—and to write—such pieces. Everyone wants to write the great soaring eagle novel, a mighty hosanna. But small pieces, occasional pieces, visiting your computer the way the unassuming junco visits our feeder, that's a blessing, too.

K IS FOR KARYATID, the stone ladies holding up the pantheon (sometimes spelled with a C, I admit). Now, stone ladies in stone draperies are fine for Greek monuments, but characters made of stone, who move stonily, who wear stone clothing, are stone boring in a book.

Lively characters do lively things, not lie about and mope or sit and stare catatonically at the fire, wishing life were different. Leave the stone for the statues.

L IS FOR LOMOTIL, the medicine that helps sufferers of diarrhea, but where is the medicine for sufferers of logorrhea, which is diarrhea of the mouth? We writers have to be very wary of logorrhea. Not all words are equal to others. Words like *thing* and *nice*, for example, are simple symptoms of logorrhea; adverbs galloping across the page are another; run-on sentences a third. Let me give you an example.

> It was a nice, lovely day, the wind from the east, bringing swiftly the salty, briny smell of the wine-dark sea and its ancient memories of salt grass and shining stones and the crossed legs of tiny children crying pitifully because of the sand, which had gotten high up into their private places, making them itch and scratch until red lines like blood appeared all over their small bodies.

Whew! It's actually hard to write that way. Yet if we apply verbal Lomotil to that simply awful sentence—yes! it's one sentence—we get this:

> It was a lovely day. A salty wind came from the east, carrying with it childhood memories of all those sunny days at Virginia Beach. There my brother and I had snugged down into the sand until we'd become a mass of itch, scratching hard enough to leave red lines like back roads all over the map of our skin.

See? Shorter sentences, crisper, more personalized. Better all around. If you can't hear the difference, read the two out loud.

M IS FOR MOWGLI, the feral child raised by wolves who ends up king of the jungle in Kipling's *The Jungle Book*, an instructive study in how to write a character. Mowgli begins as a powerless, naked child stalked by a fierce tiger and rescued by a mother wolf. He learns all the languages of the jungle and as a grown-up takes his place atop the hierarchy of jungle life. But he is still—when dealing with the greed and cynicism, the arrogance and deception of humankind—that naked, hairless, helpless cub. He is, as Montaigne says, two souls in a single breast. We both sympathize and aspire with Mowgli. We can see him both close and far away. He should stand for all our main heroic characters, his twinned existence a template for great characterization.

N IS FOR NEGLIGEE, which shows enough and doesn't tell a damned thing. Come on—do I have to spell it all out for you?

O IS FOR OCCUPANT, that unknown cipher who gets so much junk mail. Don't write Dear Occupant prose, designed to appeal to everyone and offend no one. Strong prose should provoke, rouse, challenge, incite. Otherwise, why write?

P IS FOR PERSON FROM PORLOCK who interrupted Samuel Taylor Coleridge while he was writing "Kubla Khan," or so he said. Taking a quantity of opium,

Coleridge fell asleep in his chair and dreamed a great poem of about three hundred lines. When he awoke, he began writing but was "called out by a person on business from Porlock, and detained by him above an hour." "Kubla Khan" runs only fifty-four lines, not three hundred, and by its author's account, was never finished. But poet Stevie Smith wrote a poem of her own, inviting the Person to come interrupt her, to get her out of her thoughts. One verse goes:

> I long for the Person from Porlock
> To bring my thoughts to an end,
> I am becoming impatient to see him
> I think of him as a friend ...

Though some critics say that Smith is really writing about longing for death, I will take her at face value and say: I agree. Sometimes we writers need such interruptions, to shock us into new ways of thinking, seeing, hearing, feeling. Be your own Person if none is available. Stand up, stretch, take a walk or a bath or a cup of tea. Play with the children, shop for groceries, see a friend. Don't become so enmeshed in your writing, so enamored of it, that you can no longer see it. Interrupt it. And don't feel guilty as you do. Who can say that the three-hundred-line poem Coleridge dreamed might not have been a weary and dreary exercise? We know that the fifty-four-line "Kubla Khan" is a masterpiece.

Q IS FOR QUAHOG, a particular kind of clam found in temperate and boreal waters on both sides of the North Atlantic. Now, an ordinary writer might just mention someone walking along a New England beach, passing by broken clamshells. But a better writer will particularize, letting the reader really see the jutting, rocky shore; the spikes of salt grass; the tide pools filled with brown rockweed and starfish; the red Irish moss; and a lone, beached, broken-apart quahog rotting in the sun.

R IS FOR ROCKS, the ones on either side of a rough voyage. As writers we have to make that safe passage between the jagged stones of high art and the crags of pure storytelling. Our (c)raft has to pull us effortlessly through.

S IS FOR SALMON, who leap up waterfalls, fall back, leap again. The ones who won't quit finally make it to the upper waters to spawn. And isn't that a nice, easy moral story for writers, never mind that after the salmon spawn, they die! It's not a perfect metaphor for writing, of course. Some of us who keep trying never do make it. Even if we reach the spawning pool. The average earnings for freelance writers is four thousand dollars a year. Hardly a top-of-the-falls number. But if you *don't* keep trying, you've no chance of making it at all. Some smart aleck is about to remind us of Emily Dickinson. But I think most of us would rather be published in our lifetimes than simply lauded posthumously. (And remember, she wanted that, too, and sent out poems to editors and friends, until strangeness overtook her completely.)

T IS FOR TOP DOG. I want to remind everyone that as we chase after the Top Editor, Top Agent, Top Publisher (do we deserve any less?), we should still keep one eye always on the assistants. They are the ones who actually get things done. They make the phone calls, set the schedules, remind Mr./Ms. Top Dog about appointments, send the letters/revisions/copyedited manuscripts/checks out. And most important: Today's assistant is tomorrow's Top Dog.

U IS FOR UNDERWEAR, which should be cleaned and darned even if no one ever gets to see it. So should your prose (and grammar) be respectable, even though no one is ever again going to force you to parse a sentence or identify a gerund.

V IS FOR VERONICA, one of the spectacular passes with a cape that a toreador does on his way to dispatching a bull. But if I took up a cape without practice and without a modicum of skill, the best I could hope for is a goring. So why do thousands, perhaps millions of people take up writing and with great sweeping phrases produce verbal veronicas? Why do celebrities? Beats me. But what you see after that is a whole lot of bull …

W IS FOR WHACK FOL DE-DADDIO, the granddaddy of ballad nonsense syllables sung—I have always assumed—when the minstrel forgot a whopping great section of his song. Too many writers pad their writing with the same sort of nonsense, acres of product placement and metrosexual mantras, as if they, too, have lost the plot.

X IS FOR X-ACTO KNIFE, that razor-sharp implement used by artists and illustrators to cut away the unnecessary stuff from a picture. Would that we had such a tool. Oh right—we do. It's called the delete button. Use it early and often. Especially on modifiers that end in -ly.

Y IS FOR YENTA, the Yiddish word for a gossipy woman who always sticks her nose into other people's business. But surely gossip is what feeds the writer. We peek through keyholes, listen at doors, meddle in the lives of our characters. Without gossip there would be no stories. So, be a snooper, a sniper, a yenta. Wear the babushka with pride.

Z IS FOR ZOUNDS! one of those wonderful exclamations that shows delight, approval, astonishment, and satisfaction, the perfect way for a story—or an essay—to end.

Now, not in my alphabet, but two words and a phrase which, alas, are at the top of the publishing hit list these days. And which we, as writers, have absolutely no control over.

The words are B for *branding* and C for *celebrity*.

Branding is the concept brought over from Hollywood, in which the publisher can make dozens of similar books about a particular character and so identify it to the public. The books become their own special ... um ... brand. Certain authors—Tomie dePaola, Eric Carle, Stephen King, Anne Rice, John Grisham—produce such easily identifiable books; they are their own brands. Clifford the Big Red Dog and Curious George and Arthur the Aardvark (or is he an anteater?) and Babar are all brands. Harry Potter is the ultimate brand.

Celebrity is totally Hollywood. Celebrities write books, especially children's picture books, overnight (as Billy Crystal said he did) or because there are no good books for children available anywhere (as Madonna said she did), and they get enormous advances and suck up all the promotion budget and available oxygen. They also get on *Oprah* and the *Today* show and Jay Leno, promoting their books.

And shame, shame on the publishers and booksellers who go along with this nonsense. But no blame on the public who buy it, because—to be honest—most of them are not book buyers anyway.

The phrase is "vertically integrated synergy." It means at its core that the major big multilayered international corporation that happens to own your publishing company wants to find other ways to make money off your book. So they want the publisher to buy a book that can be used in multiple ways, all within the larger corporation's many outlets—movies, TV shows, bed sheets, book bags, video games, a line of children's clothing, product placement, jujubes named after your characters, toilet paper with the book cover emblazoned—you name it. What the music business calls *merch*. As in merchandise. Just be sure your contract gets you a piece of the action, which has, in any event, become more important these days than the literature.

Now, not to end on a sour note, I want to remind you that the sins of the publishing company are on its own head. You and I must write as honestly and as well as we can, because in the end only we are responsible for our own sins. And our own stories.

So what have I left out? *C for characterization. P for publication. A for awards. D for dollar amount. OP for out of print.*

But this alphabet—and the earlier one—is only a beginning. And my own.

15   It's your turn to write your own alphabet. Like writing any story, you may be surprised at what you find there. You might also be illuminated, changed, and charged by what you discover. We write not just to show off, not just to tell, or only to have written.

We write to know ourselves.

FINAL INTERLUDE
A Wish From the Winter Queen

As I walk into the winter of my days, I am often too warm. My thoughts come easily, my nouns do not. I remember old songs and forget the names of friends. I have enough money to buy a castle in Scotland but not the knees to mount the stone stairs.

Aging is oppositional. The soul reaches for higher things as the rest of the body succumbs to gravity. This is not what they mean by *gravitas*, but I guess I am stuck with it.

What I do have, though, is time. Not enough to write all the books I want to write, nor read all the books that accumulate on my shelves, on my tables, on my floors. But time enough to sit in the garden and watch the magpies fight the gulls for the moldy bread I have just tossed them. I suspect there's a meaning there, some metaphor about winter, but I cannot quite grasp it.

In Scotland, a nursing home is called an Eventide House. That appellation is so much more appealing, for "evening tide" is how I am feeling these days. The waves of the past wash over me, reminding me of rougher earlier seas, when I had three children in quick succession and book writing was something I did between diaper changes. Or perhaps it is "the even time of life," and that, too, has its points. The seesaw has stopped going up and down, the heart beats at a slower pace, the eyes have time to rest on beloved objects. I am what I am, and at peace with it.

I think of so many women before me, dead in childbirth, worn out by housework, farm work, undernourished in both body and mind. Had I lived in all those romantic times, I would not have been a Winter Queen, but perhaps a merchant's wife, keys clanking at my side, till the first miscarriage undid me with blood loss. Or the child I carried to term turned upside down and killed me. That I did not die of either of these, or the lack of thyroid, or the burst appendix or the tubular pregnancy of my later years, is a miracle of modern medicine. That I can publish my writing, vote, keep my own money, run a book imprint, teach in college while married, and on and on, simply marks me as a late twentieth-century, early twenty-first-century woman.

If I had another life to live, I'd run for high office. Or learn to paint. Or take acting lessons. Or learn astronomy, archeology, and anthropology. But I chose writing early, as well as poetry and music. Enough for this lifetime, enough to take me into the winter with plenty to do.

So here's a wish from the Winter Queen for all of you: May you choose well those things to carry you into the even tide of your own lives. Make a raft of those choices, a raft that will slip easily through the stormy seas, where the waves are wild and bright with foam. And may you come at last, as I have, to safe harbor and a welcoming shore with many books to hand, those you have written and those you hope to have time still to read.

INDEX